The Night at the End of the Tunnel, or Isaiah Can You See?

Mark Greenside

The Night at the End of the Tunnel, or Isaiah Can You See?
Mark Greenside

© 2018 Mark Greenside
Cover design by Kim Thoman

ISBN-13: 978-0-692-06021-6

Weasel Press
Manvel, TX
http://www.weaselpress.com

To My Political Mentors:
Ken Dolbeare, Harvey Goldberg, George Mosse,
Jim Rowen, and Stuart Scheingold,

With Thanks and Apologies

Table of Contents

Part I

Jeremiah Isn't a Bullfrog

It was the best of the worst of times, the worst of the best of times, Ouroboros, Ubu, the beginning of the end of the beginning, but I didn't know that then. It was 1979, and I thought I still had a future, which is why I'd come to New York: to prepare myself. And I did—but in a way nobody in his right mind except Leo could have possibly predicted.

I was at the time a virgin, an orphan, a lapsed Catholic, a twenty-one-year-old-small-town-in- Missouri valedictorian with a bachelor's degree in the humanities and a scholarship to study literature, and I was looking for a place to live. In the three long weeks I'd been searching— thanks to rent control and no one ever giving up their apartment even after they were dead—the only places I found that I could afford were public housing projects in the South Bronx and Harlem, where there was a waiting period of fifteen years, and the Y, where I currently resided and where a trio of not-so-wise men and a transvestite with a mustache had tried to have their way with me. Needless to say, I was dispirited, had just about lost all hope, when from out of the void I heard a tune: someone was humming the "Battle Hymn."

I looked up. Sanitation workers were recycling garbage from their truck to the street. I looked down. A homeless guy gagged on a Happy Meal. I looked further down. From inside an apartment, a finger— Leo's finger—pointed at some oddly shaped words scribbled through the dirt on the window: *Furn Apt Fr Cheap.* I was amazed, indeed, overjoyed, and as I descended each step, my hopes rose as the humming grew louder: I was certain I'd be getting a deal. I knocked on the door. No answer. I knocked again, louder. Still no answer. I opened the door.

"Hi," I called, unable to see a thing.

"Ninety-nine a month. Utilities included," came the reply from the dark.

I ignored it, stepped forward, and walked smack into a wall of hundred-degree heat. It was eighty-five degrees and sunny outside, and this guy had the furnace on. It made me glad the utilities were included. I waited for my eyes to adjust to the gloom and looked around—at the holes in the walls, frayed and exposed wiring, hanging pieces of ceiling, torn linoleum floors, and orange-crate décor. Nailed to one wall was a colorful, crayoned, hand-printed sign that said Hello Dali. Taped to another was a New York City Civil Defense Evacuation Map with circles, arrows, and what I hoped were food smudges. Beneath it hung an illuminated etching of Savonarola at the stake. Stained *Playboy* calendars, yellowed *Daily News*, and hundreds of ladies' underwear ads littered the floor. Anybody else would have looked at that place and seen only its drawbacks. But not me. I saw the three not-so-wise men and the mustachioed transvestite waiting for me at the Y. Besides, a dozen years of Catholic school had taught me to live like a martyr, die like a saint, and never succumb to the obvious. So even when I stepped forward, turned the corner, and saw Leo—tall, gaunt, unshaved, with bug-eyes, smiling a hellion grin—wearing black slacks, a black suit coat, black socks, white shirt, and a red, white, and blue American flag tie tied around his neck like a noose, all of which smelled of mold or compost or worse, even that didn't get to me. Nor did the brown and green U.S. Army camouflage ski cap perched on his head or the yellow EPA hazardous-waste slicker hanging from his shoulders. All they told me was that he needed help, that he couldn't live alone, that he was a preacher or a patriot seriously gone amuck, or a moron. I thanked my lucky stars, Saint Jude, Uncle Sam, and Adam Smith. How else could I have gotten a midtown redevelopment zone apartment for ninety-nine dollars a month?

"I'll give you seventy-five," I said.

"It's not what the market will bear."

The lucidity of his response surprised me. "It's not habitable," I said. "It ought to be condemned."

"Ha! Shows what you know." Leo laughed and waved an official signed and sealed New York City Inspection sticker right under my nose. "Besides, it has a view."

This I found hard to believe. I walked to the window and looked up. All I could see was the sidewalk and people's shoes. "What view?" I demanded.

"There!" Leo screeched. "There!" as he pointed with one hand and grabbed at his crotch with the other. "See!"

I saw right up a lady's dress. I waited for her to pass, turned around, and gazed at the apartment once more. Then I remembered I was a liberal and a humanist— and that Mother Teresa was living with lepers in India and my summer-school classes began in three days. So, closing my eyes and gulping—and hoping in my heart of lapsed bleeding hearts that Leo wasn't contagious and I was choosing the lesser evil—I said, "I'll take it," and I put out my hand to shake. But Leo was nowhere in sight. He had returned to the darkness and was once again humming the "Hymn." "See you, roomie," I waved. "I'll be back tomorrow." He hummed louder, and as I left, he broke into song: "Mine eyes have seen the coming of the *gory* of the lord." I stopped. Stiff. Frozen. Goosebumps played leapfrog all over my skin. "Nah," I said. "No way." Not even *he* would say something like that.

>>>

Less than twenty-four hours later, when Leo volunteered to show me around the neighborhood, I realized he probably did.

"Button up," he said. "It's cold out there." He already had on his camouflage ski cap and yellow EPA slicker.

I looked outside. Steam was rising from the sidewalk. "I don't think so," I said. "It looks balmy."

"Not that kind of cold. I mean *cold* cold. And put your collar up."

That time I didn't object. I just did it. But immediately I started thinking about moving.

"See that building over there?"

"Yes," I said, impressed. "It's a late Raymond Hood," and for a moment I thought I had misjudged Leo, that maybe he was an architect or an urban planner, an environmentalist, some kind of bohemian *artiste* or critic who happened to be temperature-sensitive or had some sort of endocrine problem….

"Don't go near it."

"What?"

"Don't even look at it."

I could hardly believe my ears. "That building is at least thirty stories high, not to mention some fifty-odd years old and a historical landmark. Why should I not go near it?"

"It's International Modernist crap. Bowwow house. Take Ninth Avenue. Avoid Eighth. Walk on the somber side of the street."

That was it. Right there, in mid step, among the homeless commuters and picked-over garbage, I stopped. Leo stopped, too. He removed a joint from his pocket, lit it, toked once, twice, three times, squashed it out on a mangled fire hydrant, put it back in his pocket, and said, "Let's move. That way we'll be harder to hit."

"Right," I said and clammed up, thinking that would deter him. But it didn't. He just continued to catalogue. "See that organic food store on the corner with people waiting in line to get in? The health department's closed it six times. Keep away from this fence. Lady was walking down this street a month ago and a rat came out and bit her. Cross over. Avoid that manhole cover. It's blown three times in the last two years. That old lady by the lamppost selling incense. He's a cop. Sells the best damned crack in the city. The apartment behind him. State owns it. Hookers work it. Twelve-year-old slit her own throat there just yesterday...." Leo then paused to survey and smiled. "Boy, this neighborhood is terrific. It's reaffirming. One of the most advanced in this whole doomed town."

At the time I thought Leo was crazy. I thought he was one of those halfway people who couldn't be in and shouldn't be out, and the only thing crazier was that I was with him. Not just with him but *living* with him. Right then and there I decided to move. I headed for the corner building to find a *Voice*.

"Hey!" Leo screamed. "Whattya doing!"

I was so startled I jumped. For a second I thought the manhole cover was about to blow. Then I remembered who I was with and kept moving.

15

"Not there!" Leo yelled. "Don't go in there!" I stopped and turned around. Leo was standing in the street blocking traffic, bouncing on his toes, looking and pointing up. I looked up too. Everything was where it should have been. I turned to take another step, but Leo stopped me. His face was flushed and he was breathing hard, all but out of breath. "Don't you know about this building?" he wailed. "Windows pop out when it storms... Windows..." he pointed... "Pop out..." He raised his hands and made a pushing motion... "When it storms...."

"Are you nuts," I blurted, "are you crazy?" and immediately realized I had said the right thing, which was the wrong thing to say at the time. "Leo, Leo, Leo. It's sunny. It's warm. It's eighty-five degrees. It's *spring*. There's not going to be any storm."

"Freak storm... It happens... Summer of '55... It happens, I know...." He kept repeating this, shrieking, while leaning against an uprooted lamppost and banging his forehead with his palm. "Freak storm... Diane, El Nino... I know...." Even the bag ladies were paying attention. Two homeless vets in uniforms began to applaud. Never had I been so embarrassed. Never had I felt so small. Truly, this was one of Leo's finest hours. One of his finest, for sure.

Of course at the time I didn't appreciate it. I thought it was a pitiful scene of despair. Later on that evening, though, in the privacy of my room, I felt guilty for my unkind thoughts. Had I still been a practicing Catholic, I would have said several dozen Hail Marys and made numerous acts of contrition. Instead, I stared at the poster of JFK nailed to my wall and decided to put Leo out of my mind. Why not, I figured, get even, because clearly he was out of his.

This happened before Madonna's breasts became missiles, when Saddam Hussien was our ally, Bruce Jenner was a man, and Michael Jackson was alive and black, when I was still young and hopeful and believed in *The Progressive, Nation,* and *Life.*

>>>

After that, I avoided Leo. In the mornings I left for school before he woke—even on weekends and holidays. In the evenings, if he was there when I returned, I went straight to my room, chanting, "Study, I have to study, there's so much I have to learn." And if he wasn't there, I still went straight to my room in case he should suddenly, unfortunately, appear. Then one morning I overslept and heard him in the kitchen when I woke.

I was starving and my bladder was full. I squeezed my legs together and waited for Leo to leave. I could hear him talking to himself, so I waited for him to finish. If only I could figure his schedule, I mused, I'd never have to see him again. I didn't know then that he had no schedule, only a routine, and that he was waiting for me. I got up, dressed and peed and for protection, so I wouldn't have to talk to him, I carried my *Dante* with me.

Leo was sitting at the table reading the paper in the dark. I turned the light on, opened a box of the breakfast of champions, and sat across from him on my orange crate chair. The champion on the box was Larry Holmes, but Larry was crossed out and replaced by John. I didn't know why, and I didn't care. Leo was silent, and that was enough, a very good sign, a hopeful beginning—then he spoke.

"Dante. Good."

"*You* know Dante?"

"Sure."

Suddenly I wanted to talk. "It's required for my seminar on pre-modern classics."

"Not good," Leo grunted. "*The Inferno* should be read for pleasure."

"Right. And Three Mile Island ought to be a theme

park—Fornever Land."

Leo folded his paper in half and looked up. He sat there quietly smiling, showing off his missing incisor and scratching the top of his head. "Read the paper?" he asked.

I nodded.

"Which one?"

"*Times. Journal. The Catholic Voice.*" I refused to look up as I spoke.

"Not *The News*?"

I looked up. "*The Daily News*?" Nobody but people who spoke English as a fifth or sixth language, the learning-disabled, grade school dropouts, and psychopaths like the Son of Sam read that rag. As far as I was concerned, it was on par with *The National Enquirer* and *The Star*.

"How 'bout *The Star*?"

That was it. "Have to study, work, prepare, plan...." I stood up and turned off the light. But before I could get to my room, I heard Leo call:

"Hey, Mr. Future Teacher of America! That's why you didn't know about the wind from the north and them windows and El Nino and Diane. And why you don't know this! Ten thousand species expire every year. Jeremiah isn't a bullfrog. Sid Vicious, Amoco

Cadiz," and then he started to cry.

>>>

The next several weeks were practically uplifting, as I succeeded in totally escaping Leo: not the heat, which was always on and driving me bonkers, or the smells from the twice-cooked garbage, but Leo. Inevitably, I supposed, being roommates, we were someday going to have to meet again, but I intended to postpone that eventuality for as long as I could endure. And endure I did, because every morning pinned to my door was a greeting, a little missive selected to darken my light.

For days on end I quietly read about air, noise, and water pollution, killer smog, acid rain, killer bees, the greenhouse effect, nuclear winter, People's Temple, George Moscone, Harvey Milk, Kool-Aid, Twinkies, the F.B.I., oil spills, gammarays, Xrays, ultraviolet rays, Johnny Ray, James Earl Ray, fraud, influence peddling, product unsafety, theft, perjury, embezzlement, drugs, murder, arson, bribery, hunger, poverty, simony, new diseases, old diseases, garbage, bacteria, viruses, broken sewer lines, cracked gas lines, planes that crashed, trains that derailed, buses that flipped over, leaking tunnels, worn-out bridges, falling buildings, riots, bombs, hostages, torture, nuclear waste, infant mortality, unemployment, underemployment, increases in Congressional salaries, insider trading, child molesting, buggings, buggerings, foreclosures, bankruptcies, traffic jams, illiteracy, endangered species, refugees, Jackie O's latest lover, *Mommie Dearest*, and a constant updating of the latest Nielson Ratings. *Love Boat* always finished in the top ten. Every time I read that I knew something was seriously wrong with America's vision.

I went about my days worrying mostly about what those Nielson Ratings signified, growing happier and happier every twenty-four hours I avoided Leo. Sometime in there, though, he began to do double duty, sending me his friendly little greetings in the evening as well as the morning. For several weeks I meant to speak with him about this, but speaking with him meant seeing him, and seeing him was imaginatively much worse than anything he could pin to my door. At least that's what I thought until the night I came home and found a frightening story about poison-gas experiments the C.I.A. had been conducting right here in Manhattan's subways— on the 1 Line!

"Leo," I said, crumpling the article in my hand, "this has to stop."

"It won't," he grinned. "It will only get worse. Look

21

at this." He calmly toked on a joint and reiterated a litany of disasters. "A postman in the Upper East Side is refusing to deliver all mail to the Whitney as a matter of conscience because his porno photos weren't accepted for the Biennial and Mapplethorpe's were. A father in Midtown shot his son in the head for forgetting to send a Father's Day card. A doctor in Chelsea performed 133 unnecessary hysterectomies this past year to pay her daughter's tuition to Notre Dame. And now this! On the subway! Somebody is shooting people with arrows! Can you beat that? Now there's not only dirt and gum and filth, discarded newspapers and candy wrappers, the smell of sweat and piss and cum, windows that won't open or shut, lights that flash on and off at random, doors that jam, graffiti that's heartfelt and vulgar, spit and snot and a toothless, mustachioed Miss Subways staring at me like a young blonde Truman Capote on the make, not to mention they're raising the fare, and now this, too, to contend with, a guy running around with arrows...."

"Stop it, Leo! Stop it!" I screamed. "Enough. No more. I've had it. If the world out there is so dangerous, then stay in the apartment where you'll be safe...." He stopped me with a look of utter derision.

"You've got to be kidding. One out of three injuries

takes place in the home."

I had to admit he had something there.

>>>

The next time I met Leo was by accident. In those days, *whenever* I met Leo it was by accident. Even in the apartment. It was a resplendent fall day. The sun was beaming and I was returning home from my classes, trying to appear oblivious while also looking around for a guy with a bunch of arrows, because as Leo so benevolently informed me, two more people had been hit—when all of a sudden I saw him. He was standing at a bus stop, dressed all in black with his American flag noosed-tie, army camouflage ski cap, and yellow EPA hazardous-waste slicker, covetously caressing a Brim decaffeinated billboard that had been inspirationally assisted to read Grim.

I looked away in disgust. When I looked back, he was scrambling down Lexington Avenue with a newspaper covering his head, hugging the buildings and admonishing everyone in sight. Three Hare Krishnas and a cripple scurried out of his way, a blind boy's seeing-eye dog pulled the boy into traffic for safety, and I J-walked across the Ave and hid behind the police car that had collided with the bus that had swerved to avoid the boy. It was unbelievable. There goes the future I said to myself and automatically made the sign of the Cross. Even then I remember thinking, Wow! What a reprobate! The man's a natural repellent. Imagine what he could do if he put his mind to it. Imagine what he could do if he had one! Right then and there I decided to move. Ten hours later, I told him.

"Leo," I said, "I'm moving."

"You can't."

"What do you mean I can't?" I thought he was taunting me, knowing I had nowhere to go.

"You signed a lease."

"A lease? Are you crazy? I never signed a lease."

"Uh-huh," he smiled. Then he went to his room and came back shaking a piece of paper in front of me. "See."

I grabbed it away from him and looked. It *was* a lease, signed by Gus T'Amato, Leo Solomon, and me. "Who's this guy T'Amato," I screamed! "I don't know any T'Amato!"

"He's a lawyer," Leo smiled. "It's legal."

"*Legal*! I'll show you legal! This is *America*! This is *fraud*! It's forgery! It's... It's *wrong*!"

"So sue me," Leo shrieked, waving his arms around the apartment. "Get your own shyster lawyer. Take me for all I'm worth."

>>>

All right, so Leo is a bit odd. Quixotic. Well, not quixotic in the normal sense of the word. Let's say negative quixotic. A postmodern Don Quixote. Besides, he has his good points. For one, he speaks English. For another, he's never around.... That's what I thought of him then, and it was how I planned to explain him to my friends. Only I didn't have any friends. Until Jean.

Jean transferred to N.Y.U. from West Virginia State. She was one of those educational opportunity students from Appalachia who looked like she walked right off the set of *Deliverance*: flat-chested, tow-headed, bow-legged, over-bit, hare-lipped, acned, and scarred, with a mole the size of a quarter hanging from the back of her neck. She was also sallow and slightly deaf. "The Milton midterm's tomorrow," she said. "Why don't we study together?"

"Great," I said and meant it. It was the first time anyone had spontaneously asked anything of me other than spare change or the time. "Meet you at your place at seven."

"Yes, it would be heaven, but there's no way we can do it at my place. I live in an all-girls' boarding house."

"How about the library?"

"Too noisy. What about your place?"

I was afraid of that, but there didn't seem to be any way to avoid it. I just hoped Leo wouldn't be there, and thankfully, he wasn't. We studied until two A.M., when Jean yawned, and I said, "Why don't you spend the night?"

"OK," she said, and closed her books.

Anyone else and I would have been excited, but not with Jean. As far as I was concerned, she was about as sexy as a fork. Besides, for the past seven hours we had been studying Milton, whom no one but Leo would grant an X rating. Within a few minutes, each of us was sound asleep and snoring.

The following morning I woke up exhausted and alone to the sound of strange noises emanating from the kitchen. Immediately, I got up and dressed and went out to protect my new friend. By the time I arrived everything was quiet, heads down, sullen. I could only imagine the worst: Leo had started talking about manhole covers or popping windows, guys with arrows, muggings, the C.I.A. in Iran, Bert Lance.

I didn't learn until much later that in less than five minutes he had gotten inside her pants. Had I known, I would have been disgusted. I would have thought each of them was probably the first living thing without eight legs or wings to touch the other. Still, she was my friend, my only best friend! And it was a rotten, low-down, marvelously contemptible buddy-fucking kind of thing that Leo did to show me the true meaning of fellowship... "Let's get out of here," I said to Jean.

"Milton," Leo mumbled as he noticed my book. "Good. *Lost* is better than *Found*."

"Right," I said, and pushed Jean out the door.

In the hallway Jean turned to me and said, "He's weird."

"Yes," I explained, "Leo is a bit odd. Quixotic. Well, not quixotic in the normal sense of the word. Let's say negative quixotic. A postmodern Don Quixote...."

Jean laughed. "A Non Quixote, that's good."

And for the next several weeks that's how I thought of him: as a postmodern Non Quixote, my own little Apocalypse Now.

>>>

And so it went. Leo and I nonverbally agreed to

27

circumvent the stigma of relating and left each other alone. What mostly passed between us were clippings.

Leo's clippings, of course, were more of the same. Ground Water Tainted In Thirty-Eight States. Viet Vets Living In Forests. Nestle's Kills Kids. Nuclear War Is Winnable. *Love Boat* Contract Renewed.

My clippings reached for a higher plain. Leo's came from *The Daily News, The Enquirer,* and *The Star.* Mine came from *The Times, The New Republic, Nation,* and *Life.* Mistakenly, I was attempting to introduce Leo to things that were uplifting, moral, and comforting, things he knew nothing about. I gave him a review of *Da* to show him decent theater was well and alive in the Big Apple. "Nope," Leo grunted, "Da-da." I gave him an article on Immanual Kant hoping to engage his intellectual side. He returned it with a huge angry X ripped across the page and a note. "Don't give me Kant. I'd rather have dogma instead." Next, I tried religion, a story about faith and its successful application to drug users, and how it changed their lives. "Won't work," Leo shook his head. "Marx was wrong. Opium *is* the religion of the masses. Read *The News.*" Closer to home, I told myself, I've got to find something that hits him. I finally found it in *Life,* a story about Three Mile Island and how all of the systems worked to avert disaster.

"Lemme see," Leo winced.

I gave him the magazine and waited as he solemnly sat on his orange crate and read the article word-by-word. When he finished, he folded it in half and sat there, hunched over, looking more depressed than usual.

"See," I grinned, "Some things *do* work as they're supposed to."

He shook his head in despair. "The *pumps* worked, the *cooling* system, the *mechanical* things...."

"That's right."

"*People* didn't. Don't you see! The problem was *human* error, and *we* can't be fixed. We're beyond repair. History is the future. Nothing will ever change."

"Jesus Christ," I said, pulling the *Life* out of his hands, "you're hopeless."

"I know," he said, "I know."

>>>

One night I found myself in the apartment cooking dinner. I was scraping an inch of boiled-over chicken potpie gunk from the overused toaster oven because the gas line to the stove was leaking again, when I realized I didn't know much about Leo. I knew he was on disability. He told me that when I first moved in. But he never told me what for. For a while I thought it was physical because of the clothes he wore outside, and because in the winter he turned off the heat, and in the summer he turned it on. My still patriotic self wanted to believe it was war related—something to do with Agent Orange—that somehow it messed up his internal heating. That's why I put up with it for so long. I didn't know then there's nothing in this world he'd fight for. Later, I thought it was mental, some sort of developmental or emotional wreck. It wasn't until much later that he told me his uncle is an I'm Ok—You're OK Transactional Analyst who was begged to death by his mother to write a letter to anyone certifying that Leo was nuts. She owed him, Leo told her, for bringing him into this world—and if she didn't do it, he'd move back into her house. That's what got him on disability, and between that and rent control, the Salvation Army and me, he survived.

So there I was, alone in what passed for a kitchen, eating beans out of a can, trying hard not to touch that globule of fat those Heinz people legally pass off as pork, thinking of Leo, when I heard a key slide into the first of the five locks that bolted the door. For a moment I was almost pleased to see him. Already I was becoming inured.

"Leo," I exclaimed, "h-how ya doin'?"

"Huh."

"How was your day, old roomie? What'd you do today?"

In a flash, his face was three inches from mine. His fingers gripped the sticky crumb-laden table and his knuckles turned eyeball white. Sweat popped out of his forehead. The veins in his neck turned miraculously Renoir blue. He looked like a Francis Bacon painting come alive. "Whatchu mean?" shot out of his foul-smelling, rotten-toothed mouth.

I ignored his demeanor, scooped up a steaming spoonful of beans, held them over his knuckles to ensure detente, and said: "I only meant since you're not working or going to school, I was wondering what you did all day."

"Museums."

"Museums!" I was astonished. "*You* go to museums?"

"Sure."

"The Met, the Whitney and MOMA?"

"Yup."

"And the Guggenheim and Natural History?

"Uh-huh."

"Really!"

"Libraries, too. That's where I read Dante and Milton."

"No kidding."

"And buildings."

Ah, I thought, there's the old Leo: out searching for popping windows, crumbling balustrades, sagging mansards, loosened gargoyles, fraying wires, corroded pipes, frozen elevators, documenting further urban and structural blight....

"The Old Knickerbocker, the new Port Authority. Places like that." He smiled.

It was beautiful. Downright inspirational. I was envious. Here I was a slave to my studies, practically living in the library stacks so I could maintain my C minus average and stay in school, and there was Leo, wandering the City, a free man, experiencing some of the most celebrated works of humanity. The only thing I couldn't figure was how he could spend so much time amidst these intellectual and cultural treasures and still be so morally and spiritually broke.

>>>

Not long after that I ran into Jean at the Central Park Zoo.

"What are *you* doing here?" She looked away from me as she spoke.

"Same as you I guess. Cutting classes and enjoying the weather.... Haven't seen you around much."

"Been busy. You know, school and all." Her gaze, like a beacon, focused on an incredible sight. Not more than thirty feet away was this thing wearing an upside-down green Hefty bag with holes ripped out for its arms and eyes, bouncing on its shoeless feet, clapping its hands, screeching, "E..E..E..E...." At first I thought it was a piece of performance art—like everyone and everything is garbage—but then I saw the yellow slicker under the Hefty bag.

"Hey, that's Leo."

"Where?" Jean said, looking in the other direction.

"Over there—creating a spectacle."

It was true. People thought Leo was part of the zoo. Better than the zoo. Kids were gaping at him and pointing. One little girl even cried and screamed when her mother tried to pull her away to see the bears. I walked over to him.

"Skipping the old museums today, huh, Leo?"

He said nothing.

I shrugged. "You remember Jean, don't you?"

He and Jean shrugged.

I could have kicked myself for coming over and saying hi. Still, since I was standing there and had already publicly admitted knowing him—and especially since Jean was still there—I asked, "So what are you doing?"

Leo looked at me as if *I* was nuts, then began screeching again, "E..E..E...."

"Watching the old monkeys, huh?"

More nothing.

In disgust, I turned away. *"Look! Look! Look!"* Leo screeched, grabbing the sleeve of my coat and pulling me back. "They're playing with themselves."

I glanced at Jean in embarrassment. She smiled, then turned away. "Leo," I endeavored to explain, "that's not their normal behavior, they're doing that because they're confined."

"And what are we?" he yelled. *"And what are we?"* Then he ripped off his Hefty bag and threw himself down in the dirt.

Instinctively, I gave him the finger. It was the first time in my life I had ever done such a thing in public. I immediately felt remorse. But Leo beamed and Jean laughed and a family of homeless people threw popcorn at me while a guy dressed completely in plaid pointed and called me a geek. I was mortified. I saw myself becoming like Leo.... Isn't that funny? I was afraid of becoming like him, and now, of course, I'm much worse. Life certainly has its high points.

>>>

One cold, wet, cloudy, dismal day, in what I can only describe as a devil-may-care act, I accompanied Leo down Canal Street. I was walking three or four steps ahead of him, trying to disassociate myself from his presence, because on that day he looked worse than normal. Along with his usual disarray of clothing he had a set of pink and white Deely Bobbers waving from the top of his head, a Ray-gun-for-President bumper sticker pasted to his pants, and he was singing, singing as loud as he could, "I Will Survive." Everyone was looking at him as if he was crazy — on Canal Street! He's a lunatic, I told myself, pulling three more steps ahead, a one-track mind with an eight-track personality, a one-man doomsday machine, a lost object.

That's what I was thinking, when coming towards me I saw one of Leo's fellow travelers: a weirdo in green and black Viet Nam-era combat boots, and a soiled and stained, obviously previously discarded, belted and epauletted 1960s C.I.A. look-a-like trench coat. On his head was a World War I leather flyboy's helmet with earflaps flapping and goggles pulled down. One of the lenses was painted red, white, and blue. The other was shattered and cracked. I had no idea how the fellow could see. He was slowly making his way towards me, pushing a shopping cart overflowing with bags, careening it off of innocent bystanders, sidewalk displays, and parking meters. If that street had been a pinball machine, the guy would have scored a zillion points. And behind him, I saw, also concerned about the weirdo, was an attaché-cased, wing-tipped, button-down-shirted, Brooks Brothers, London-Fogged, Republican business-type exec with an American-flag lapel pin. He was pacing the weirdo, observing his movements and looking over his shoulder from left to right. I thought he must be out searching for deals. Well, I figured, if Canal Street is good enough for Mr. Bank of America, then Canal Street is good enough for me, at which point I, too, began scrutinizing the goods. I was looking for a Happy Face to give to Leo or a poster of Mother Teresa. That's what I was doing when suddenly I heard a scream. I looked up. The weirdo was in the gutter.

At the top of his lungs, he wheezed, "Stop... Thief... I'm a veteran...Help... Halt...Mugger... Stop...."

I couldn't figure out what was happening—a weirdo

in the gutter, screaming for help. It happens every day. But then I saw Mr. Bank of America racing toward me, grasping one of the weirdo's bags. Nobody was doing anything to stop him. Everyone was clearing a path. Well, the sight of the helpless screeching, now-bleeding-from-the-belly weirdo and the noninvolvement of Mr. and Mrs. John Q Public was more than I could bear. "I got him," I called, and leaped forward in an attempt to intercede—and slipped on a piece of pizza, fell onto a sidewalk sales counter, and got entangled in a mass of fish netting a Chinese salesman was trying to sell to a Vietnamese family. "Leo," I called, seeing Bank of America approaching him, "Stop him."

Leo stepped aside.

"Good idea, Leo. Stick out your foot. Trip him."

Leo folded his arms.

"Leo," I wailed. "*Do* something."

Leo smiled, then crossed his legs and sat lotus-legged on the sidewalk and watched as Bank of America went right past him.

"I can't believe you did that," I said, after the Vietnamese cut me out of the netting.

Leo grinned.

"Leo," I hissed, "get up." I was afraid of making a scene.

"What? What's the matter with you? I didn't do anything."

"That's right," I started yelling. "That's right, you didn't do anything at all. You could have stopped that guy and instead you sat down on the ground and did nothing."

"There's nothing to do."

"Nothing to do! Nothing to do!" I was so excited I was jumping. "You could have stopped the guy, that's what there was to do...."

"Everything's been done."

"What?" I was incredulous.

"Everything's been said. Everything's been done. There's nothing left to do. All we can do is wait."

Suddenly I became aware of the people surrounding us. I also heard the weirdo groaning in agony. Out of the corner of my eye, I could see him in the street, hemorrhaging, but I was determined to beat Leo at his game. I wasn't about to let these people, these innocent bystanders, this Silent—soon to be Moral—Majority go away thinking Leo was right. "Look, Leo," I said, calmly resorting to reason, "If there is nothing to do because everything has been done, then you damn well could have done something, which by your logic is exactly the same as nothing. One act is as meaningless as the other." I looked around. I knew I had him. The crowd was nodding its agreement, and Leo was very, very quiet.

"Well, Leo?" I goaded.

"I didn't feel like it."

The populace broke out in applause, and I immediately thought of Bartleby. I had recently read the story and was very much impressed. The professor had told the class that Bartleby was the end of humanity as we'd known it, the beginning of modern man, the forerunner of existentialism, and an omen of things to come. Naturally, when he said that I thought of Leo, and now there was this, too, to consider. Things were beginning to fall into perspective, and for the first time really, I dimly perceived there might be more to Leo's perversity than dementia, that there might just be some assumption behind his acts. From that moment on, I watched him.

>>>

I didn't have long to wait. A week later, I came across Leo again. In those days I still thought our occasional meetings were just poor timing, erroneous luck on my part. I didn't know yet that he had carefully planned them. So on that day, when I saw Leo on my campus, I was shocked.

My Poe class had just ended and I was cutting across the mall to the library. In the center of the mall was a rally. I kept walking. Rallies meant nothing to me. I was in college to learn. But there, bobbing up and down in the front of the crowd was Leo. My first reaction was to run away. However, having so recently decided to watch him, I ambled over to see.

In the beginning there was not even a word. With the exception of Leo, the crowd was fairly stable. On the makeshift platform stood a woman with red-white-and blue-streaked hair. She was bedecked in black leather, had what must have been a five-pound chain around her waist, a razor-blade crucifix hanging from her neck, and a safety pin punched through one ear. She was carefully arranging her notes. I shut my eyes to avoid seeing more, then opened them abruptly when she bellowed:

"Dooooooom."

"Dooom," Leo repeated.

"De-struc-tion."

"Deconstruction," he clapped.

"Armageddon."

"Yes," Leo wailed, "I'm-a-get-on."

"The end of the world."

"Oooooh, yeah... The end... The end... The end."

"Sinners...."

"Y-E-S!"

"You are going to die and rot forever, forever, you're going to burn...."

"Yes, yes, burn, burns, double bubble, toil, and trouble."

"Hell, damnation, purgatory, awaits you... Satan...."

"Ooooooooow, The Inferno... *Gory* Hallelujah! *Isaiah,* can you see?"

"Only this man," shouted the speaker, pointing at Leo, "Only this man understands the fate of his state...."

"Yes, yes, I do, I do, I do, I do, I do...."

Three hundred years of religious freedom had resulted in this, a Jonathan Edwards and Mom team. No wonder the elders opposed the vernacular mass. "Come on, Leo," I said, rushing in, grabbing his collar, and yanking. "Let's get out of here."

"Huh."

"Let's go. You don't belong here."

"What? Why not?"

"Because you're a Solomon, Leo, a Solomon..." I was whispering so no one would hear. "Those people, they're, they're... Christians. To them you're a Christ killer, a killer of Christ, you killed Christ...."

"I killed Christ," Leo shouted, "I killed Christ."

"That's right, sinner," roared the speaker. "You killed Christ."

"I killed Christ," he began to chant. "I killed Christ."

"Jesus Christ!" I implored. "Holy shit! Let's get out of here before they stone us."

Safely at the library, I tried to explain to Leo the difference between him and them. "Leo, those people aren't like you."

"No?"

"No, Leo, they're Christians."

"So."

Clearly I would have to explicate. "Well, for one thing, they believe in eternal afterlife."

"Close." He smiled, then shrugged.

"Close?"

"Close enough."

"Close enough to what, Leo? To what?" I was shrieking.

"To infernal afterbirth, you idiot. Don't you get it? Can't you see? Infernal afterbirth, unoriginal sin— that's all you need to know to survive. Shits float. Here," he said, holding out an apple in his hand. "Bite it."

For a second, I was nonplussed. Then suddenly something clicked, one of those "Aha's" pop psychologists like to write about. A few years earlier I read a book about Treblinka, which left me pretty well steeped in German concentration-camp terminology. So what I did in that instant was put (a) Leo, together with (b) that terminology, and came up with the word *Sonderkommando*, which was how I now saw Leo: a man willing to walk among the dead to ensure his own survival; truly a spiritual hussar, a Jeremiad, a member of the Futilitarian elite. Realizing that, I smiled and said, "I see."

Leo smiled too and nodded.

Together we walked home in silence, the only sound between us the chewing on the apple we shared.

>>>

Clearly, my resistance was wearing thin. Leo's presence was taking its toll. I no longer viewed him as a certifiable bedlamite, but as postmodern and future man. I was beginning to understand that he courted the repulsive in order to survive. Still, I wasn't too keen on being around him. I thought: if he represents the future, who needs it? And its corollary: then what the hell am I doing in school? Neither of which question I wanted to answer, but Leo knew that, as he knew that my guard was down. That was why on New Year's Eve—my feeblest point in months—he decided to give me his *weltanschauung* of doom. As soon as I heard it, it made sense. It explained America's decaying cities, guys with arrows, the right-wing Republican regurgence, and *Love Boat's* lasting success.

The holidays were dismal, more so than usual. We had no ornaments and exchanged no gifts. The only season's trimmings were three cards: one for me from Benjamin Jeffries at my orphanage and two that Leo claimed for himself. One was a mass-produced dot-matrixed picture of the manger from an insurance company in Wisconsin. The other was a calendar card from a local funeral parlor. Both had been direct-mailed to the wrong address. I felt awful, like I always did on New Year's Eve—I hadn't yet learned that living worst was the best revenge. I was alone and had no idea where Leo was, and it was probably for the best. Had I known that he was humping Jean—and had done so repeatedly since that first night in the kitchen—I definitely would have gotten sick. As it was, I wasn't feeling too great, which is why I chose to remain in the apartment, luxuriating in the illicit heat, polishing my shoes for the new year. The only good thing about the night was Leo's absence. If I was miserable without him, imagine how much worse it would be if he was there. At which point, of course, he returned.

"What in hell's going on here?" he boomed, slamming the door behind him.

"What! What!" I jumped, thinking the building was about to collapse or the guy with arrows had followed him home. "What!"

"The heat's on."

"That's right, Leo, the heat's on. And it's staying on." I felt brazen. "I've had it with freezing my ass in the winter, not to mention roasting my nuts in July."

Disappointed, Leo shook his head. Sullenly, he walked across the room and lowered himself onto his orange crate. His hands began wringing his pants. "What about nuclear winter?" he whined.

"What about it?"

"How will you ever be ready?"

I had to concede he had me there.

"Look," Leo said, closing his eyes as he spoke, "when the big one comes, there will be lots of heat and fallout. The heat will melt the permafrost, and the fallout will block the sun. Don't you see? Summers will be hotter, winters will be colder, and only those whose bodies have become acclimated will survive. You ought to read *The News*."

Except for that last line it all made sense to me, which is why I didn't object when Leo stood up and turned off the heat. I simply resumed polishing my shoes as Leo went into his room. Suddenly, though, I felt lonely, more lonely than when I had been alone. "Leo," I called, "let me borrow your portable radio?"

I had never actually seen Leo's radio. For that matter, I had yet to visit his room. But I knew he had a radio because late at night I heard him listening to the Connelrad alerts.

"Here," Leo grunted, staring at me suspiciously.

I turned it on and rotated the dial searching for something I liked. Leo stood over me and watched, then returned to his room in a huff. Towards the end of the band I found what I wanted: a Beatles retrospective, the Beatles from A to Y. "Yeah, yeah, yeah," I started singing along. I felt so good I wanted to dance. I actually got up and began to shuffle. About five minutes later Leo came back into the room and settled himself on my orange crate. I sat down on his. I knew if he thought I was having a good time he would become upset. But when I saw him tapping his foot, I thought he was getting into it, so I jumped back up and shimmied.

"Gimme that," Leo snarled, snapping the radio out of my hand and switching the dial. "If you have to listen to music, listen to this...."

"What's that!" I yelled, pushing my fingers into my ears.

"The Sex Pistols. Punk. Johnny Rotten. That's where it's at—No future, the future."

Defeated, I crumbled to the floor.

"Now what!" Leo screamed over the noise.

"I was listening to the Beatles."

"So."

"So they're great, that's all. They're a joy. One of the few things that make me happy."

Leo smiled as I said that, turned off the radio, and said: "With charity for none and malice towards all, a house that is subdivided will fall... Abraham Lincoln."

"What the hell does that mean?"

"The Beatles will never play together again. Goo Goo Goo Joob.... I am the eggman."

"Leo, that's not funny. That's not funny at all."

"'The blood-dimmed tide is loosed, and everywhere, the ceremony of innocence is drowned. And what rough beast, its hour come 'round at last, slouches towards Washington to be born?' W.B. Yeats."

"It's not Washington, Leo, it's *Bethlehem*."

"You'll see. In time, everything is impossible. It's better to be too soon than too late.... Leo Solomon."

Wow! A roommate with a philosophical bent. Then, to fortify myself and spite Leo, I went to the kitchen and renewed my subscription to *Life*.

"What are you doing?" Leo yelled. "You've got life. What you don't have, I just told you, is time—*See!*"

I looked around and didn't see anything. "See what?"

"Nothing."

"Nothing?"

"That's right."

"What's right?"

"Nothing."

"Nothing's right?"

"That, too."

"What too! What's right! Jesus Christ, *what's* nothing!"

"Tomorrow, and the day after, and the day after that... All nothings...."

The year was over. Ten thousand more species had died. The new, new Richard Nixon was making public appearances again, again. Ronald Reagan was ahead in the polls. Margaret Thatcher became the not-so-prime minister of England. Ayatollah Khomeini returned to Iran. The Soviet Union invaded Afghanistan. Disco and one million Cambodians were dead. The Eighties were here—and Leo was almost content. The last is what worried me first.

Part II

Eau de Tombe

Leo had a secret, several secrets, in fact, but I was too busy to notice. All my time was spent studying. In the mornings I awoke early and was the first to enter the library, and in the evenings I was the last to leave. The result was something akin to a hangover. I became tired and weary and weak: a somnambulist. The good news was Leo's clippings had totally ceased. The bad news, though, was much worse. What I now got came with Leo's personal touch—The World According to Solomon.

"Hey! Mr. Humanist! Mr. H & H—Heartfelt and Hopeful—take a look at this!"

"Not now, Leo, I'm tired. I've got midterms to study for."

"There's a new rapist in town."

"Big deal," I groaned. "There's always a new rapist in town."

"Not like this. This guy has a new shtick."

"Right."

"He wears a mask."

"They all wear a mask."

"Yeah, but he takes his off...."

"C'mon, Leo, I'm tired."

"After he does his shtick."

"I'm going to bed."

"You know what he does?"

"I don't care."

"He tapes their eyes shut with glow-in-the-dark Duct Tape, and *then* he takes his mask off. That way he can see them and they can't see him. Pretty neat, huh!"

"Forget it, Leo, it won't work. I'm exhausted."

"Then he covers them with jam and licks them all over their bodies."

"No kidding."

"Yeah, I can't believe they caught him. Some guy at Walgreen's spotted him stealing a case of Shmucker's and the police identified him from a pubic hair stuck in his teeth."

"Not to worry, Leo, not to worry. The guy will hire the best lawyers his money can buy, and he'll get off with six months or less. They'll tell the jury he's a Duct Tape safety expert who got stressed out and became a little too zealous and he's really sorry. Or they'll use the old junk-food Twinkie defense and claim he was hypo or hyper glycemic and out of control. If all else fails, they can go the government agent route, subpoena thousands of pages of top secret documents about illegal spying on Americans from the F.B.I., then claim to reveal this information would compromise national security and go for an Executive Pardon. Anyhow, next time he'll remember to floss...."

As soon as I finished I was aghast. I couldn't believe I'd said those things. I only said them, I told myself, because I was tired and less talk meant more sleep. That's what I repeated to myself again and again as I stood there silently dazed.

Leo, though, was whimpering. Suddenly he began punching his head. "Knew it!" he wailed. "Knew it! Knew it! Knew it! Should have been a lawyer instead."

Instead of what, I was afraid to ask.

>>>

The following morning it was more of the same. I woke up beat and went to the kitchen for a drink.

"Hey," Leo yelled, "don't do that!"

"Don't do what?"

"Don't dirty that glass."

I looked around the apartment. Leftover food was everywhere. Roaches had taken over the sink. The garbage was as high as the counter. "Are you nuts?" I screamed. "Are you crazy? Spiders are dying in here from the dust! Do you hear me, Leo? Spiders are dying in here from the dust—and you don't want me to dirty a glass?.... What's that smell?"

Leo smiled and held up a can of lemon Pledge.

"You're cleaning!" It was something I had never seen him do.

"Nope, polishing."

I looked around again, thinking that maybe in my current blur something new had been added to the decor. All I saw were the usual orange crates: orange crate chairs, orange crate tables, the orange crate couch. "What needs polishing in here?"

"The orange crates."

"You're polishing orange crates?"

"And hastening the greenhouse effect."

"Ah!" I said, figuring the only way to silence him was to go along with his numbskull ideas. "Good idea. Let's buy aerosol everything. And Styrofoam! And non recyclable bottles and cans and non biodegradables and plastic too! That way, by doing nothing, by just living as regular, normal Americans, eating and drinking and cleaning and polishing, not to forget using the heat and dumping all this garbage, we can play our own special part in further depleting the Eco structure."

Leo was dumbfounded. Never had I seen him so joyous. I proceeded to heat up a Styrofoam-packaged frozen lasagna dinner and dirty two glasses, one cup, three plastic spoons, and a plate. Why not, I figured? It took so little to please him, and the atmosphere was so large.

>>>

Frankly, I didn't know how Leo could do it. I was becoming narcoleptic. Yet no matter what time I left or what time I returned, he was always there to greet me. One morning at about four, I was awakened by a terrible nightmare. I dreamt I heard Leo laughing. Stricken, I lay in bed. Then, when I had almost fallen back to sleep, I heard the same horror-filled noise again, like a death rattle. Gingerly, I opened the door. Leo was sitting on my orange crate reading *The Star* by the light of the blinking Bud sign. On the floor, in front of him, was a cover story about John and Martha Mitchell in *The National Enquirer*. I tried to sneak away, but he saw me.

"Ever hear of Billy Joel?"

"C'mon, Leo," I whined, "it's late."

"Billy Joel, ever hear of him?"

What else could I do? I answered, "Of course."

"Well, don't listen."

"Right. Now can I go back to sleep?"

"No."

I trudged over to Leo's orange crate and sat down. "All right, Leo, tell me why is it I shouldn't listen to Billy Joel?"

"Because he's a phony, that's why. An imitation. A namby-pamby. All pap, no smear." Leo grinned and rattled.

I yawned.

"It's the outlaws, not the crooks, you want to pay attention to. Little Richard. Chuck Berry. Young Elvis. Johnny Rotten. Sid Vicious." Then he stared right at me. "Never trust anybody with two first names," he said.

"Leo," I smiled, "after living with you, I don't trust anyone at all."

"That's good. That's good," he clapped. "Don't trust

anybody with two first names even more."

"You got it. Whatever you say. Good rule. I'm with you. Bad night."

>>>

The only things I had to look forward to were my exams and Dr. Roberts' reading from *Macbeth*. On the morning of the reading, I awoke with my head abuzz. The evening before—at three a.m.!—I was forced to listen to Leo pontificate about Sanyo, Sansui, Toshiba, Hitachi, Yamaha, and Akai. His concluding comment: "The only fidelity left is Hi."

"How true," I said, "how true." I hadn't the slightest idea what he was talking about. It wasn't until much later—at five o'clock!—that I finally realized Leo was talking about stereophonic sound and not the Japanese High Command. So to prove to him that I understood, just before I left for school I walked over to where he was sitting, pulled the cold hot dog he was chewing out of his mouth, and repeated: "Remember, the only fidelity left is Hi."

Leo gave me the thumbs up sign and said: "And the only heroes remaining are sandwiches. Buy high, sell low. Every loss is a gain. A Bull is a Bear by a different name. Dearth First!"

"Right," I said, and slammed the door shut behind me.

When I got to Dr. Roberts' class, the lecture hall was full. Towards the front of the room, I spotted an empty seat next to Jean. I walked over and sat down.

"Lots of people," I said.

"Yes," she said. "Everybody comes out when old man Roberts reads."

"He's that good?"

"Yes, Gielgud, Olivier, Richardson. He's performed with all three."

"Wow! So where have you been keeping yourself lately?"

"Oh, you know... I've been busy." Then she blushed. I knew it was a blush because the color of her face became different from the color of her zits. "H-how's Leo? I haven't seen him since... Since that day at the zoo." That's what she said! Can you believe it? I tell you, that Jean is something else: she's as good a liar as she is ugly; a treasure of unearthly delights. Of course, I didn't know that then, so I answered, "Leo is Leo, a hazard to all that is right."

Jean giggled. "I'll say. But I've been worried. The last time I spoke with him, he sounded awfully tired."

"Sure. He ought to be. He's preternatural. The son of a bitch never sleeps."

"Oh, no!" She sounded shocked. "That's not what he told me. He told me he's been so tired he can't go out. Every afternoon, he naps."

"Every afternoon!" I blurted. "Every afternoon!" I stood up. "Every afternoon...."

"Have you finished your soliloquy?" It was Dr. Roberts.

"Yes, sir."

"Then shut up and sit down."

I did, but I was so nervous that I knocked my books, then Jean's, onto the floor. When I finally finished straightening things up, Dr. Roberts began to speak. From memory. The little bugger was amazing. He had to be eighty years old. He couldn't have stood more than five feet three. Yet the guy had the lungs of a bagpipe. Words came out of his mouth as if powered by a bellows. As he spoke, his whole body shook, right down to the thin little metal legs of his walker. He was going along splendidly, rapidly approaching the part of Banquo's ghost when suddenly from beneath the curtain there appeared a blood-splattered, sheet-covered ghoul. Slowly, it crept towards Dr. Roberts. The audience was really excited. And so was I—until

I realized the blood was tomato sauce from the frozen lasagna dinner I ate in bed the other night, and the sheet was mine. I leaped out of my seat to warn Dr. Roberts, but in the commotion I made, he stopped and stared at me and gaped for the full two seconds it took Leo to reach him and tap him on the shoulder and shriek, "BOOOOOO!"

The last time I saw Dr. Roberts, they were carrying him away in a gurney. He was still gaping at me, only now he was also drooling, trying to raise his right arm, muttering and sputtering, "FFFF." At the time I thought he was giving me the finger, which, under the circumstances, I can truly respect, although I don't think I honestly earned it. It wasn't until later in the day, when I went to take my exams, that I discovered that FFFF was my grade. In all my classes. Leo had told the custodian who captured him that he was my roommate and that the plan to do in Dr. Roberts was mine. And since he left the sheet with my name on it as evidence, they believed him. I went straight to my student government representative to protest, but she hadn't been seen in months. "And even if she was here," the secretary told me, "she certainly wouldn't see *you*." So I went to the Dean of the School of Law, who was a world-class Lawyers Guilder. As soon as he heard my name, he punched me. "Roberts," he said, "was progressive."

>>>

What can I say—that I felt anger and chagrin? Of course, I did. All of my studying had been for naught. I returned to the apartment that night with the intention of talking to Leo. It was something I had never done.

"Leo," I said, "I've been thrown out."

"Yaaaaahooo," he yodeled.

"I said I've been thrown out. I've been ejected from school."

"It worked! It worked!" He leaped in the air, came down on my favorite orange crate, and smashed it to smithereens. "My plan worked!"

"What plan?"

"My secret plan! My secret plan!"

This really took me by surprise. I thought I knew Leo fairly well, and there was nothing I knew that led me to believe he could plan. "What plan?" I demanded. "Huh!"

"Do you remember New Year's Eve?"

"How could I ever forget."

"Remember that I came home early?"

"Another of life's little pleasantries."

"Well, I came home with a resolution."

"A resolution?"

"Yes," he clapped, "a resolution. I resolved to get you thrown out of school."

As soon as I heard this, I laughed. I doubled over in hysterical giggles. My eyes watered. My stomach ached. It was the funniest thing I had ever heard. I was choking, it was so hilarious. Finally, I managed to gasp: "Leo, you fool, a resolution does not a plan make."

"You're here, aren't you?"

I threw him against the stove. "That's why you were always awake and waiting for me..." I punched him in the belly. "You were keeping me tired..." I kneed him in the groin. "And off guard..." I split his lip with a frying pan. Then I stepped back, looked at him, saw blood and teeth all over the place, and kicked him again for being so pitiful. After that, I shuddered and broke down. "Why, Leo, why? School was so important to me. It... It was the only thing I had going.... It was my hope, my faith—My *future*!"

"*That's* why," he choked. "That's why." Blood seeped out from his gums, his hands were holding his nuts, and his head was in the garbage. "I wanted you to be like me."

>>>

Some people would have harbored a grudge, but not me. Catholic school had seen to that. Besides, ever since I was a kid and witnessed my mother carving my father and then carbon monoxiding herself, I have known that every silver lining has its cloud. I guess that's the kind of guy I am. Expect the worst, and you won't be disappointed. In this world of future shock, it's important to know some things will always be the same.

The next several months were satisfactory. For one thing, I had my scholarship money for the year and no intention of returning it. For another, there was Leo. Being out of school left a gap in my intellectual development. Sure, there was plenty to read, but what? After forty-five Harlequin Romances, you've read them all. And what did I care about "How To" books: Pritikin this, Scarsdale that; how to make money; how to repair.... As if changing anything had ever changed anything at all. I read political thrillers, personal exposés, and murder mysteries, but none were as compelling, cogent, or earnest as what Leo read to me from *The Daily News*.

That's how it was. Leo sat on his orange crate reading *The News,* and I sat on mine, listening and luxuriating in being and nothingness. Until one night—in the middle of a story about a priest who specialized in fondling acolytes with the names of the apostles—Leo stopped reading, stood, went to his room, returned with a book and thrust it into my hands.

It was *Civilization and its Discontents.* I bent the cover back and snapped the binding.

Leo smiled. "There's more," he said, "when you finish."

And that was how I began to read again. Leo filled my intellectual breach. No longer would I be just an egghead. Theory and praxis would become one— which was why, a few weeks later, I got a job.

>>>

"Leo, I want to work."

"Don't do it!" he shrieked.

"But I *need* to," I said, and then I explained about theory and praxis. "Life is loss. You know it. I know it. The books you give me to read know it. But except for you, I have nobody to practice on. I need to get out in the world and be productive."

Leo picked at his nose and belched. I knew he was seriously thinking. I went on while the pickings were good. "What better way to do it," I asked, "than to work in a family restaurant? I saw a help wanted sign."

Leo squinted. His eyes began to water. With a twist of his thumb he ripped out a giant bloody goober and held it up to contemplate, then he brought down his fist and pounded the table: "Freebies on the eats!" he demanded, as the goober flew through the air.

I leaped, trying to spot where it landed. "You bet."

"Ok, try it. Who knows, maybe you won't even like it."

>>>

Two days later I went to work, and it was terrific. I yelled at everybody. "Wat'chu want!" "Can't you read!" "We don't have no stinking gorgonzola—only *American* cheese will do!" The best one, though, was the guy who wanted tamari sauce for his turkey-bacon-avocado sandwich. "Are you nuts?" I screamed at him. "You want tamari today?" I also got to spill things on people, deliver the wrong orders, and ridicule the out-of-towners. On the very first day I was even lucky enough to be able to give a family from Indiana wrong directions. They came in and didn't order anything—just wanted to know how to get to the Cloisters. I told them to take the subway to Lexington and a 125th and walk. The owners, Mom and Pop Windsor, adored me, and so did their flatulent daughter, Irene.

The first time I picked up an order, she cut one and said, "That one's for you, big boy." The second time I went back there, she patted my rump. And the third time, she said, "Wanna see my scars?"

"Not now, Irene. I have to deliver this rat-turd-tuna-dolphin combo."

"Oh," she said, disappointed, then let loose with a trumpet of gas.

"All right," I said, "make it quick."

She smiled a smile that had more teeth missing than Leo's, and she proceeded to unbutton her blouse. All I could think was, my first breasts, my first breasts, I am about to witness my first breasts. I was very highly expectant. Irene, however, was having trouble as her grease-laden fingers kept sliding off the buttons. "Help me, big boy," she gurgled, "Give big momma a hand." Nervously, I loosened the top button. With restraint, I undid the next... Beneath her blouse her huge breasts loomed like Kilimanjaro.... The third button came easily undone. Irene was breathing hard now. In one swell swoop she inhaled, then exhaled, and farted, shooting buttons four, five, and six across the room. Her blouse, though fully unbuttoned, clung to her sweating skin. I pulled it away from her body, stepped back, and stared. With her eyes bulging and her tongue protruding, Irene reached up behind her and unclasped what had to be at least a half dozen stays. Then, as quick as she could, she lifted her bra and revealed what I could only describe as mammoth. All I could do was gasp. There are Grand Tetons and there are grand tetons, and these were the grandest tetons of them all. Her nipples were the size of mushrooms. Growing out of them, around them, and over them was a forest of hair so thick Tarzan could have swung from any one of them and never lost his grip. And beneath those hairs, spreading out unevenly, incidentally, desultory, from the mushrooms of her nipples as far as the eye could see, were pock marks, little blisters that had already started to pop.

"See," she said, placing both of my hands on one of her breasts. "See my scars." I gulped. "My titties got splattered by the french fries."

From that moment on, we were a pair.

Every time I cheated a customer, she hugged me, practically breaking my back. And if I made someone wait a long time or deliberately brought what they didn't order, she would guffaw and guffaw and cut one. She made me so miserably happy.

Finally, the time came when I knew we were going to do it. "Let's do it," she said."

"Oh, boy!" I was really excited.

Her place was out of the question. She lived with her mother and father. That left my place, and as much as I'd grown accustomed to Leo, I didn't want him to be there, especially since I hadn't yet told him about Irene. As soon as I opened the door I saw him. Immediately, I slammed it shut.

"Irene, my roommate's in there. I think you should know that he's strange. He's not dangerous—at least physically—but he's very, very strange."

"Goody, goody," she glowed, turning each of her four chins a different shade of pink.

"You sure?"

"Uh huh."

"Ok, here goes." I opened the door and announced, "Irene, this is Leo. Leo, this is Irene," and waited for the worst. But everything went ok. We sat around the crumb-covered table drinking Kool-Aid out of almost empty Miracle Whip jars. Leo scowled; Irene guffawed and farted; I watched. It was a pleasure to see the two of them getting along. Leo told Irene horror stories about the City and the nation, and she told him what's in the food he eats and what really happens to leftovers. After about twenty minutes of getting acquainted, Leo looked at Irene and smiled, then he turned to me and said:

"She sure is ugly, isn't she?"

"Leo," I shrieked, "cut it out."

"No, I mean it. Really."

I was about to split his lip again, when I happened to gaze at Irene. She was crying. Tears formed rivulets in the creases of her cheeks. Snot hung from her nose. "Baby, baby," I consoled, "it's ok, it's ok...." At which point she stomped on my foot, flipped over the table, and hurled herself out the door.

"Good night, Irene...." Leo sang, then turned to me and said, "Moves pretty fast for a big one."

If I had been able to walk I would have killed him. Instead, all I did was lie there, hold my foot, and moan: "My first woman, my first woman, she would have been my first woman," over and over again.

The next day I went to work afraid that Irene would have told her parents and I'd be fired on the spot. When I got there, though, everything appeared copasetic. Pop waved me a big hello and Mom called me over for a piece of apple pie. Irene was nowhere around. When I reached Pop's side, he put his arm around my shoulders, smiled, and jammed his fist into my kidney.

"So you don't like my Ireney?"

"I do, I do, I swear."

He stomped on my toe, the same toe Irene had hit the night before. "She's not good enough for you?"

"She is, she is, I swear."

"You abused her?" His fingers chewed into my neck.

"No, yes, I'm sorry."

"You shoulda taken more advantage." Then Pop buried my head in the egg salad and stomped on my other foot. "Now get outta here, ya bum, you're fired." I looked over at Mom for help. She waved, then came charging at me, and ran me out of the restaurant and down three blocks swinging a moldy three-foot giant salami, screaming, "Next time finish what you start."

>>>

After the Windsors, I had had enough of the world. I returned to the monastic life of books. For the next several months I stayed in the apartment and read. It was on one of those nights while I was reading *The Air-Conditioned Nightmare*—or maybe it was *The Best and the Blightest*—that I discovered another of Leo's little secrets. I went into the kitchen to dirty a Styrofoam cup and cut my foot on a piece of glass, and, as I bent to remove the slivers, I discovered what I should have already known. Stuck to the floor in some boiled-over bean juice was a tiny piece of paper. I picked it up, noticed the four stars Leo marked along the top, and read:

> M/W/F 46 Wants to be serviced
> by young stud. Anything! goes.
> Hubby gives his approval. Park
> Avenue residence. Must be into
> environmental concerns.

How can I express what I felt? Revulsion, I suppose, and antipathy. It brought back all of my concerns about Leo as a weirdo and added one more: sex crazed. I was furious. Not only was I not getting any—had never gotten any, thanks to Leo—but he was out lining it up. Piqued as I was, I then did something I never thought I would do. Had it been anyone else I would have been ashamed, but since it was Leo, I thought of it as just desserts. I sneaked into his room to look for the evidence to nail him.

I opened his door and was astonished. Aside from his smell, the room was clean. Spotless, in fact. And Spartan. I went to the bookcase and perused the titles and authors. Most of them, I was proud to note, I had read in the past few months. Above the bookcase, I saw a life-size photograph of Sid Vicious in leather and studs. I wouldn't have recognized him then, but the picture was signed, "Fuck Everything, Leo... Sid Vicious." The other photo, the one over Leo's bed, I recognized immediately as Geraldo and Oral Roberts. This bothered me. Nothing I had seen indicated the depravity for which I longed. Then, on a hunch, I peered under Leo's bed, and there, neatly arranged in piles were dozens and dozens of sex mags: *Tits and Ass; Ass; Jugs; Black Jugs; Bound and Gagged; Leather; American Stud; Girl on Girl; Spanked.* My first thought was Sid Vicious must have known Leo better than I did because everything imaginatively fuckable was there: boys, girls, old men, cripples, transvestites, fat ladies, transsexuals, dogs, sheep, donkeys, and one magazine that was filled with nothing but photos and ads for sex aids. Clearly, this was something we were going to have to discuss.

"Le-O," I charmed, when he walked into the apartment. "Where've you been?"

"Museum."

"Oh, yeah," I smiled, "Which one?" My hands were behind my back.

"Whitney."

"That's nice. Educational... And what's this?" I thrust out my hand with the ad.

"An ad."

"I know that, Leo. What's it doing here?"

"I cut it out. I thought it was kind of sweet. You know how concerned I am about the environment." He was giggling.

"And what's this?" I screamed, waving a copy of *Bound and Gagged*. "And don't tell me it's a magazine."

Leo sat down and looked at me. I could tell he was weighing things, trying to decide what to say, and if this was the time to say it. After a while he spoke: "Historically speaking, two things always seem to happen whenever an empire defaults. There is a decrease in the hope and faith of its inhabitants and an increase in selfishness and sexual exotica. To survive, you have to go with the flow.

I was awestruck. In those three sentences Leo succinctly summed up everything I had been reading. It was magnificent. Still, I was miffed at him for lying. "Well, that's just fine and dandy, but what's all this crap about going to museums and old buildings?"

"What crap?" Leo shouted, and stood in an angry huff.

"Crap, Leo, crap. Just admit it, you were lying."

He smiled. "No I wasn't. I go as often as I can. Next week I'll take you...*If* you pass the test!"

"Test? What test?"

"The Seder test."

"Seder? As in Passover?"

"No," Leo beamed, "Seder as in Pass Under, a walk on the Oscar Wilde side of town."

>>>

"First, we eat," Leo announced.

On the table were all of his favorites: a Mama Celeste pizza supreme; Mrs. Paul's fish sticks; a Banquet TV turkey dinner; cold Kraft's macaroni and cheese with ketchup; plenty of Styrofoam and plastic; Wonder Bread; Jell-O; and Kool-Aid. During the feast, amidst the flickering of two dozen candles, we sat on our orange crates and talked about books. It was, I thought, a ridiculously easy test.

"Finish Celine, Jarry, Eliot, Yeats, and *Candy*?"

"Yup."

"All of Henry Miller, Beckett, Nathaniel West, Drew Pearson, and Oscar Wilde?"

"Uh huh."

"Genet, de Sade, Reage, Bataille, Gibbons, Kafka, Kissinger, and Moliere?"

"You got it."

"The tragedies, Dadaists, Surrealists, Absurdists, and Rachel Carson?"

"All done."

"Derrida, Freud, Duchamp, Spengler, Popper, Bukowski, and Friedan?"

"Right."

"*Finnegans Wake, The Book of Job, All the President's Men, Dispatches, Candide, The Pantagruel, Gargantua, Catch-22, Maus*, and all those *Mad Magazines* and *Mr. Naturals*?"

"Yeah!"

"Ok," he said, finishing off the macaroni. "Now let's get on with the questions."

"The questions?" Suddenly, I was worried. My stomach turned. I couldn't even finish my Jell-O. "Who asks them?"

"I ask. You answer. Let's go."

Nervously, I waited as Leo licked his plastic plate clean. Finally, he looked up, folded his hands, and began. A sliver of green Jell-O hung from his nose.

Q. Why are we different from all other people?

A. Because we accept our fate. More than accept it. We expect it. We are the vanguard of decline.

Q. Why, then, don't we rape or steal or shoot at people with arrows?

A. Because you are what you do and nothing that you do really matters. One act is as meaningless as another, and everything has already been done.

Q. What is it, then, that we do?

A. We encourage and appreciate what is.

Q. And what is?

A. Doom, deconstruction, and chaos. The night at the end of the tunnel. The chickens coming home to roost.

Leo paused. I was so scared I thought I was going to pee. I watched him stroke his chin, then rub his nose, discover the sliver of Jell-O and eat it. "Those are the four questions," he said. He said it so solemnly I was certain I had flunked. "Now, to honor Mark Van Doren, you may ask one of me."

My mind went blank. Everything I thought of sounded trite or false. What is it I want to know, I asked myself? What is it I really want to know? Then it came to me, the question when answered that would fill in all of my blanks. "Who made it this way, Leo? Who caused it and why?"

"Everyone," he smiled.

"Everyone?"

"Yes, with their craving for more and better. It was the ruthless pursuit of goodness that caused it, goodness and hope: the capitalists with their faith in free markets, the invisible hand, and endless prosperity, and the Marxists with their dreams of a withered-away state and universal equality; all religions with their belief in a better world to come, and all nations and political parties for promising what they wouldn't want to deliver even if they could; and families too, and lovers and artists and philosophers, and all those who gave with everything they had, *especially* their reasons. In postmodern America this was first revealed to us in the late 1950s by the publication of William Burrough's *Naked Lunch* and Ike's lie about the U-2. This was also when the Giants and Dodgers moved West and the Yankees started to lose."

What could I say? He was brilliant. Who else could have pronounced a postmortem on religion, politics, art, and baseball in one clean sweep of the tongue? Reverently I sat there waiting, wondering how I had done, and Leo, with his flair for the dramaturgic, sat there also, alternately picking his nose and sipping Kool-Aid. Then, when his nose was clean and his cup was empty, he shouted, "Ouroboros."

"Ouroboros?"

"Your desideratum."

"Yahoooo," I shrieked, "I passed. What is it? What's my prize?"

"It's in here somewhere," Leo said, standing up and clapping, then jumping up and down. "You have to find it."

With increasing glee I began to search the apartment. I looked everywhere: under the sink, beneath the orange crates, through the garbage, in my room and all of the cupboards and all of the drawers and each of the shelves, and found nothing out of the ordinary ruins. That was when I saw Leo peeking over at his room. Hesitantly, I went to the door. I remembered reading in my high school theology classes that this was part of the ceremony. I thought I was letting Elijah in. But when I opened the door, I saw Jean. She was lying on Leo's bed completely naked, with her knees drawn up and her legs spread wide, beckoning me with her pinky. I gaped. I sputtered. I moaned. Then I shut the door, spun around, and leaned against the wall for support. My stomach and everything in it was in my mouth.

"Nice, huh!"

"It's the ugliest thing I ever saw."

"You got it."

"A dog."

"Bow wow."

"I can't do it."

Leo threw me up against the wall, gripping my shirt in his hand. "Look," he hissed, "there's a lot of ugliness in all of us. You just have to be lucky enough to find it. With Jean, it's a little more obvious. She's my girl." Then he released me, opened the door, shoved me in, and commanded: "Do it!"

Only I didn't know what to do. Jean had to help me, and from the back—that is, not having to see her zits or harelip—she wasn't half bad. Afterwards, which was about fifteen seconds later, I pushed her away and asked:

"H-how was it?"

"Terrible," she growled.

"Good," I said, and rolled over to get some sleep.

>>>

Sometime during the night Leo joined us, because

when I woke the following morning, all three of us were in bed. I woke first and found my head at Jean's feet. Then she woke up, gazed at me, and winced. Finally, Leo got up. It was wonderful. We lay in bed, three hopeless romantics, counting all the wars then going on in the world. I think we agreed on forty-three, every single one financed by American taxpayer's dollars. The only difference of opinion we had was over Italy. Leo wanted to include knee-capping, and Jean and I wouldn't let him. "A maiming is a maiming is a maiming," he said, "and these are international."

But Jean argued that organized troop movements had to be involved. "Knee-cappings, ear-slicings, kidnappings, and finger removals don't make it," she said. "They're not enough. If they were, we'd have to include Newark, Detroit, and Los Angeles—and the whole *world* would be at war."

"*It is!*" Leo shrieked. "*It is!*"

I played the role of the mediator. "Leo," I explained, "in a certain abstract sort of way, you are correct, but if we fuzzy up distinctions here, we'll never be able to make any sense."

He smiled, and a moment later said, "Let's go."

"Go? Go where?

"Uptown. I told you I'd show you my haunts."

First we went to the Whitney, where Leo went straight to a giant plastic toilet and bowed five times just like a Moslem in Mecca. "Now this," he said, "is art." I walked away and looked at a disappearing, doing its best to become invisible, *White Target* by Jasper Johns. It was something I could appreciate. Then as we were leaving, Leo spotted a sign: Joseph Beuys' *The End of the Twentieth Century*. We entered what turned out to be a maze and followed it. At the end, piled on the floor, were forty-four chunks of basalt. Each chunk had a large circular disk cut out, which was removed, wrapped in felt, and replaced. Leo went nuts. He started jumping up and down and clapping. Then he fell to the floor and sniffed. "*Eau de Tombe,*" he whispered. "This is serious." I went outside and waited.

Next we went to the Met. I never saw Leo more at home anywhere—even at home—than he was walking among the detritus of centuries and centuries of ruin: Chinese and Japanese, Roman, Egyptian, Etruscan, Mayan, Greek, Indian, Aztec, and Ibo. "This is where I learned," he said wistfully, "that in time everything is impossible." The boy was almost ecstatic. Upstairs, he paused to enjoy the works of Goya and Bosch. Rarely had I seen him so satisfied—until he walked into the Modern wing and fell to the floor and began screeching, "Wrong! Wrong! Big Wrong!" It was something in blacks and browns and broken plates and antlers. "Crook!" Leo screamed. "Namby-pamby! Phony! Don't look! Bad Wrong!" I pulled him away and sat him down facing a Francis Bacon. Minutes later, surrounded by dozens of Bacon's, Leo calmed. On the way out he stopped at the Temple of Dendur and waved, "Bye-bye."

We walked across the park to the Natural History Museum. Leo wanted to visit his friends the dinosaurs. I walked with him as he went around and around the brontosaurus, the tyrannosaurus, and the stegosaurus, shaking his head and muttering, "If these guys couldn't survive, how can we?" It was a question I wished I could answer. On the way out he stopped at the evolution exhibit and sat staring at the progression of skulls and nodding. I thought he was checking things out—making sure nothing had changed since the last time he was there. "Look," he said, "scientific proof of modern man's undoing."

I looked. "What are you talking about? It's the story of evolution."

"Exactly!" he said. "Humans have turned into apes. E..E..E."

He was awesome. A zillion people could look at that exhibit and not one of them would see what Leo just saw. I pulled him into the lobby. "Now what?" I asked.

"MOMA!" Leo jumped. "I want MOMA!"

At MOMA, they wouldn't let Leo inside. The Samoan security guard stood with his arms crossed over his cask of a chest and formally shook his coconut head, No.

"I'm a taxpayer," Leo lied, "and a voter..." The guard shook no. "I have a student discount card..." More no. And this time I joined the guard. That card was mine, and Leo stole it! "...A gold card... A disability pass... A letter from my art therapist...."

"Leo," I interjected, "we're wasting our time. This place still has standards. Let's go."

"Fuck 'em," Leo said, and the Samoan clobbered him with his war club.

The Samoan and I had a good chuckle over that. Then I helped Leo out of the gutter and set him on his feet. "Where now?" I grinned.

"Times Square," Leo mumbled, then wobbled and rubbed the bump on his head.

As we approached the square, I became more and more impressed. I simply had no idea Leo knew so many people. Every hooker, pimp, dealer, wino, weirdo, military recruiter, and pretzel vendor on the Avenue of the Americas seemed to know him. It was the first time ever I really felt proud to be seen with him.

"Here it is," Leo pointed.

"What?"

"The Old Knickerbocker Building."

I looked up. Sure enough, the plaque on the wall read Knickerbocker Building. The marquee above it read: *Debbie Does Dallas* and *American Maid*. I should have guessed: the Old Knick was a porno palace.

"Which one do you want?" Leo was smiling.

"Which one what?" I didn't understand. "I thought it was a double bill."

"No," he said, and nodded in the direction of three women. One was bigger than Irene. The other made Jean look good. The third was a Nordic knockout.

"Oh!" I leaped as soon as I got Leo's gist. "That one."

"No," he said, "not Crystal"

"Why?" I whined. "I want her."

"You can't have her."

"Whyyyy?" I was already starting to drool.

"Because..." He broke into a Bojangles tap dance and sang, "'Never make a pretty woman your wife.'" Two of three women applauded.

"Leo, Leo," I restrained him, "that's good. A nice song. I like it. I do. You're terrific. But I don't want to marry her, I want to sleep with her. There's a difference...."

"Who knows," he shrugged, "One thing can lead to another."

"All right, damn it. I'll take Betty Bimbo. The one who looks like Irene."

And once again Leo was right. He never spent a better three-dollars-and-fifty cents. Betty Bimbo was worth her weight in condoms, none of which I bothered to use. That, I think, is how I got the clap, and how Jean got it, and Leo did too.

>>>

It was on the evening I came home from the V.D. clinic—or as we call it down there, The Culture Club—that Leo gave me the news. As soon as I opened the door, he yelled, "Hey, did you hear? John Lennon's been shot."

I stopped dead in my tracks and tried to read him. At first, I thought he was joking, but then I realized he couldn't be, because Leo has no sense of humor at all. Understanding that, I remained quiet. I was waiting for him to say, 'I told you they'd never play together again, Goo Goo Ga Joob,' but he didn't. He just sat there sucking on a lemon and staring at me as I stood in the doorway, searching for a response, clutching his prescription for ampicillin.

"Yeah, he's a goner. Bullets all over his body. All of them at point-blank range."

Aha! It hit me why Leo hadn't said I told you so. To him, this was more important than a prophecy. It was a test—a test as significant as Pass Under. That one measured my intellect. This one would divulge my emotional state. I was furious. Why, I asked myself, why does everything always work out for Leo? Of course as soon as I asked it, I knew it couldn't be otherwise. My anger then dissipated and became a new-found respect: I realized that Leo had a skill. That is, no matter how bad things got, Leo could always make them worse.... One minute I walk into the room looking forward to telling him he has the clap, and the next minute, before I can speak, everything I am is on the line. He was ingenious. I knew I had to be careful.

I sat on the floor to think. "I guess that means the government won't deport him now. They'll probably even make him a citizen. Hell, if this was Chicago they'd already be counting his vote."

"That's a good one," Leo beamed — "They'd already be counting his vote."

"Here's another good one," I said, handing him the prescription for ampicillin. "You've got the clap."

>>>

"Life," I said, "is a series of little murders." I was reading Hannah Arendt's *Eichmann in Jerusalem*.

"You're not kidding. Look at this."

"What?"

"Some teacher in a state boys' school was discovered to be a pederast."

"So." I wanted to get back to my reading.

"So the school board forced him into early retirement."

"Uh-huh..." A survivor was testifying about witnessing the gang rape of her daughter. "Get on with it," I said. My story, I thought, was better than his.

"So this guy—who I guess couldn't face life without a ready supply of young boys—mutilated himself and three teenagers, then razed and burned down the school. Forty-nine kids and the teacher were killed."

"All right!" I said, not even bothering to look up from my book. "Who says you can't take it with you!"

"You can't."

I looked up. "What do you mean?"

"The teacher was Benjamin Jeffries, the guy who sent you your Christmas card, and the school was part of your orphanage."

My roots! I was stunned. Up until that moment I knew I always had some place to write to and that someone would remember me during the holidays. And now, in a flash, I had nothing. I looked around the apartment and was horrified. This dump, furnished with orange crates, cluttered with debris, smelling of garbage, with a newly hung clothesline dividing the living room into quadrants, was now my home. And then, I had an even more terrifying thought: if this was home, then Leo was my family. Shaking my head, not quite willing to believe it, I didn't know what to say.

But Leo did, and it was perfect. He said, "Welcome to the newest emerging majority, kid. The World of Refugees. Tomorrow Land... You're number 800,000,001. You can't go home again."

Part III

OUROBOROS

After that, we became a team. Ronald Reagan assumed the presidency and Leo and I lived in the mire of mirth. On Wednesdays, when the marquee on the Old Knick changed, we dressed down for the 9:45 a.m. show and were the first to be seated and the last to leave. And on Fridays, we went to Bryant Park, spread the *Swinger's Directory* on the dirt and perused the personals for something that caught our fantasy, which was how we met Sal and Lou. "Here's a good one." Leo pointed.

I read: 2 Lesbos. 36 & 42. Riverside Drive. Ready for kink. Need 2 men. Call anytime. A phone number was given. "Doesn't do anything for me," I said. "How about this one?" I was looking at an ad from a fifty-year-old Upper East Side matron who would provide free tickets to a Neil Diamond concert at Madison Square

Garden to two young men if they would escort her and her daughter and diddle them during the show.

"Nah," Leo said, "Can't stand Neil Diamond. Let's call the lesbos."

"I don't know." I wasn't too keen on the idea.

"Don't be a jerk," Leo screeched, and he shoved me onto a cold, half-eaten, thrown-up burrito. "They're perfect. The phone number means they mean business. And there's no photo. Do you know what that means?" I shook my head no, then wiped the burrito goop from my hand to his ski cap and smiled. "They're a couple of real bowwows!"

Bow wow could only be considered a euphemism. Either one of them could have curled the hair of a pit bull or frightened a Doberman white. I could see that as soon as they opened the door.

"C'mon in, boys," coaxed Sal.

My mouth dropped. Talk about your alternative lifestyles! They were clothed in matching little-girl paisley dresses, had matching pearl earrings, matching red bows in their matching teased hair, matching charm bracelets, and matching tattoos—only Sal's read Lou and Lou's read Sal. Each of them weighed over three hundred pounds. As far as I could see, the tattoos were the only difference between them. I had to keep reading their biceps to determine which one was speaking.

"Well..." That was Lou.

I hesitated, then took one small step backwards for mankind, but Leo leaped forward. What else could I do? I followed.

"Sit down," ordered Lou. "We'll be right back."

I looked around. The apartment was ultramodern white, furnished in black lacquer, stainless steel, and glass. There were no books, no magazines, and no plants. An original Warhol *Dollar Sign* hung crookedly on the dining room wall. Behind the loveseat was a fish tank. In it swam a single piranha. "Leo" I said, "let's get out of here."

"Huh." His mouth was full of Cheetos.

"Let's go. They're built like a truck driver and her truck."

He smiled, showing me a mouthful of chewed-up Cheetos through the holes where his teeth used to be.

"A couple of sumo wrestlers."

He grinned.

"A butch and a butcher. They'll kill us."

Leo clapped, then swallowed and said, "I like them. They've got faces like my Aunt Martha's pug."

"Pugs," I hissed, "you can step on. These are a couple

of pit bulls. Lesbos from Hell. Human potential, they ain't."

"Hi, boys."

I looked up. Sal and Lou had changed. They were now wearing matching crotchless black leather lederhosen, matching black leather bras, and matching black leather armbands. On their feet were shit-kicking boots. Sisterhood was more powerful that I thought. Gloria Steinem, what hath thou wrought? Panzer divisions in drag.

"I'm getting out of here," I muttered, and aimed myself towards the door. Sal then strutted over to face me—I knew it was Sal because I read Lou on her arm a split second before she decked me. The next thing I knew she was carrying me over her shoulder. As I looked back I saw Leo being pummeled by Lou. "That'll teach you," she punched. "Spilling Cheetos on my carpet," she kicked. "I'm going to have to teach you to behave," she clobbered, splitting his lip and crunching his nose. For a moment there, I was really happy—until I saw the bedroom. It would have made every C.I.A. Director in U.S. history proud.

I was thrown down on what I first thought was a bed, then thought was a rack, and finally figured out was a rotisserie. My head was locked in a yoke and my hands and feet cuffed to the frame. Sal then proceeded to rotate me and slap my butt with a ping-pong paddle. On each of the first fifty rotations I was pleased to note that Lou had shackled Leo to the wall. She also had a green Styrofoam Statue of Liberty crown on his head and was pinching and goosing and punching him. Finally, before delirium, Sal quit.

"Arm's tired," she gasped.

"Good," Lou grunted. "Let's strip them."

Stripping, however, was apparently too good for us. Either that or they didn't know the difference, because what ensued was a general shredding of every stitch of clothing we had. When that was done, Sal began probing my privates. She slipped on a surgical glove, lubricated it with KY jelly and smiled. I shivered. She was going to touch me and freeze-dry my nuts. I closed my eyes and held my breath. She jabbed me with her thumb. "Hey!" I screamed. "Hey!... Not... T-H-E-R-E!"

After that, it was all up hill. My only fear—and I should have known, because I had read enough Freud to understand everyone gets what they least want because that's what they're most avoiding—my only fear was Sal would sit on top of me, so of course she did, nearly suffocating me and adding new meaning to the phrase the devil takes the hindmost. From that moment on anything she wanted she could have. I was hers for the taking—and she took. The only saving grace was as I was being ravished, I got to watch Lou abusing Leo.

"C'mon," she pinched, "move it. Get it up, wise guy, Jesus Christ!"

Honestly, I was really worried. Had Leo not gotten it up one more time I think Lou would have bitten off his dick and used it as swizzle stick. As for me, I was high on the hog. Several hours later they quit.

"It's late," Sal said, "I have the early shift tomorrow."

"Let's switch," Lou said. "This is fun."

"No. I'm tired."

Lou glared at Sal. Sal glared at Lou. Each flexed a bicep. "So," I asked, "what is it that you guys do?"

"OBGYN," Sal said, and punched me. "Lou, over there, teaches kindergarten." Sal then untied me, and Lou begrudgingly unshackled Leo, and together they threw us out with only our overcoats for warmth. As we walked down the hallway I heard one of them call the other a sow. It was followed by a scream, then another, and the sweet sound of crying and tears.

Outside, I looked back at their window. Sal and Lou were frantically dancing, hugging each other and kissing—or strangling each other to death. Leo shoved me against a tree stump. "Next time," he spat, "I get the ugly one—or else!" Then he took Lou's crown from under his overcoat and put it on top of his head and grinned. "Ain't the New Age terrific!"

>>>

During this time there was a great deal of public discussion about the economy and "America's New Beginning": supply side this, treacle down that, invest, merge, spur, deregulate. All of the papers—including *The Times* and *The Journal*—were filled with heart rendering stories about how hard it was to be rich and white in America, and how a million no longer bought what a million had bought, not to mention the minimum wage. That was why, the papers explained, President Reagan had to order the Agriculture Department to decrease the amount of food poor kids were getting in their school lunches to half a cup of vegetables instead of three-fourths, and six ounces of milk instead of eight, and why ketchup had to be considered a vegetable, and why the cost of this trimming was doubling. It was pay as you go, and it went.

"Free Lunch Over," headlined *The Post*. "Bite The Bullet," read *The Monitor*. "Somebody has to Pay," proclaimed *The Times*. "Not Us," said *The Journal*. "From Free Market to Flea Market, screamed *The News*.

It was while reading *An American Tragedy* that I had a thought:

"Leo, have you noticed that the personal ads in the *Swinger's Directory* come from the well-to-do?"

"Sure," he said. "The poor have to sell it to live. The rich can afford to give it away. Think about it."

I thought about it and it made no sense. Unbeknownst to Leo, I had taken a course in economics as an undergraduate, and the professor, in the true spirit of know thine enemy so you can hate him more, made us read Lenin, Marx, Keynes, and Galbraith. Everything I read and everything I knew told me the rich never gave anything away. Sal and Lou, I was sure, were deducting Cheetos and the dungeon as a government-approved business or medical expense and writing it off as a loss, just like the matron with the Neil Diamond tickets and Exxon with its Mideast bribes and Bill Casey, Michael Milliken, Drexel, and Merrill Lynch. The more I thought about it, the more certain I became: Leo knew nothing about economics.

>>>

Even the Old Knick was pandering economics. The marquee read *Wanda Whips Wall Street* and *China De Sade*: *See New York Lick the Pacific Rim*. "Let's go," I said to Leo. "This could be bi-lingual." Leo couldn't care less. But then he saw the raffle sign. That got him. To win, all you had to do was come closest to guessing the exact number of used condoms in a fifty-gallon fish tank.

We turned in our numbers and patiently waited, watching Linda Wong getting seriously manhandled. Suddenly the film stopped, and the manager stepped out on the stage. "Another President of the United States has been shot. This one will live. There's no need to worry, Al Haig is in charge, not Bush. And" — he paused for a drum roll — "the exact number of used condoms in the fish tank is 1503." My heart skipped. Let me win, let me win, I kept repeating. And right then and there I vowed never again to throw away anything from Publishers Clearinghouse. "The winning number from the audience is 1600, also, by the way, the President's address."

"That's me! That's me!" I was leaping for joy, ecstatic, and jubilant, as all of the regulars came over to congratulate me. All of the regulars except Leo. He just sat there, grumbling, in his typical funereal pall.

Then he stood up and shouted, "Start the flic."

During the showing of *Wanda,* I was so distracted I couldn't even enjoy watching Wall Streeters being whipped. All I could think of was my prize. I did notice, though, that my lack of ability to concentrate had no deleterious effect upon Leo. Then, finally, at last, after what seemed like an eternity, the movie ended and we went to the manager's office, where he presented me with a twenty-five-inch color RCA that had Holiday Inn engraved across the top. As soon as I saw it, I began to jump up and down and clap.

"Don't take it," Leo said.

"What? Are you crazy?"

"Don't take it."

"Why not?"

"Because," he said, "it's American. It's junk."

"Everything we have is junk!" I yelled, then calmed. "Anyhow, it's probably made in Japan."

"I still don't want it."

"Now what? You afraid it will clash with the decor?"

"Emissions," Leo wailed. "Emissions will fry my nuts."

I laughed and explained, "Leo, Leo, there's a bright side here. If your nuts get fried, then scores of future generations of Americans won't have any more little Leo Solomons to shit on."

"Mutants! What about mutants!" He was screeching. "Gene splicing. DNA... Zombies!"

"Box it," I said to the manager.

>>>

Leo and I were a team, but we were marching to different bummers. I was going out, visiting museums, hanging around the Old Knick, and becoming a Times Square luminary, while he stayed in and became a televisionary, an aficionado of all that appeared on the tube. Whenever I saw him, it was the same pathetic sight: hunched over in the corner, sitting on his orange crate, toking, with his yellow EPA hazardous-waste slicker hanging from his shoulders, U.S. Army ski cap and Statue of Liberty crown on his head, a bag of Cheetos on the floor, and a three-inch wad of tin foil scotch taped over his crotch. It got so I could hardly stand to see him.

Worse still, everywhere I went I heard, "Where's Leo?" The Samoan security guard missed clobbering him. Betty Bimbo at the Old Knick said he never visited her anymore and that he still owed her $3.50 from the last time. Even the pretzel vendors were offended. The few times they did see him, he didn't even bother to beg. He just walked right past them with his ubiquitous bag of Cheetos. It was simply too much to take. One afternoon I jumped in front of the RCA and waved my arms and screamed, "Leo, this is madness!"

"Yeaaaaaah," he said waving me aside, "he's brilliant."

I turned around and looked. Richard Simmons was leading a group of about thirty tubettes through a series of deep squats and burpies. "How can you look at this? It's abominable."

"Shhhh... Shhhh... I know. Watch this guy, he's terrific."

Not knowing what else to do, I watched. In less than twenty seconds, four of the tubbos rolled over like dead rhinos and passed out.

"See, see," Leo shouted, "I told you, he's terrific. Under the guise of building sound health and bodies, he kills them. What a gig! And brought to us live in our homes on TV."

I changed the channel, recklessly searching for something else. At channel thirteen, I stopped. A tall, balding, middle-aged man with a slight paunch and a southern accent was talking to a little black kid who, except for the pink scar that ringed his throat looked as ordinary as any other little black kid.

"What's your name?" asked the white man.

"Sha-bazz."

"Shabazz, that's a nice name. And where do you live, Shabazz?"

"At-lant-a."

"That's nice too, Shabazz. Can you say that?... Nice...."

"No, suh."

"Sure you can, Shabazz. That's our word for today... Nice."

"Turn it off!" Leo screamed. "Enough, No more. No more...." He collapsed in a quivering mass, pulled the ski cap down over his face, and began banging his head against the wall, chanting, "No more. No more. No more...." I turned down the volume.

"Want to go out?" I asked.

The ski cap and crown bobbed up and down.

"I can't hear you."

The crown bobbed faster.

"I still can't hear you." I turned the volume up full blast.

"....*Nice*, Shabazz. Say *nice*."

"Yeeess! Yeeees!" Leo shouted over the tube.

"Anything! I'll do anything! Just turn it off. Make him go away. Anything...."

"Want to go to a fuckerwear party?"

Leo lifted his ski cap, stuck his fingers in his ears, squeezed his eyes shut, and said, "OK." Twenty minutes later, after the RCA had been shut off and the color had returned to his face, I went into the bathroom, where Leo was taking a dump and shooting himself in the mouth with a can of Cheese Whiz. "W-who was that white man?" he asked.

"That was Mr. Rogers," I said, "and if you try to get out of going tomorrow he'll get you."

Leo shuddered and pulled down his ski cap. "That's one guy I need to avoid."

>>>

Getting Leo to agree to go to the party was one thing. Getting him there was another. As soon as we arrived at the subway station he balked. "BMT," he sputtered, "N..Not There!"

"Yes, Leo, it's the BMT."

"Brooklyn? We're going to Brooklyn?" He began to cry. "I'm not going to Brooklyn. Uh-huh. Not me, No way." He latched onto the banister with both hands.

"No way. Uh-huh...."

"Are you finished?"

"Nope. Not going."

"Leo, that's where the party is, and that's where we're going. Don't be so provincial."

"Nope. Nope."

I tried reason: "Brooklyn has all of the iniquities of Manhattan—and then some. I guarantee you'll feel right at home."

"No way. Uh-huh."

I tried guilt: "It was you, Leo, who said our job is to appreciate what is, and you never said Brooklyn was not." Nothing, I knew, upset teachers more than having their own words tossed back at them by a student who actually listened. I smiled in anticipation of Leo's response.

His face went white. He looked at me as I had never seen him look at me before. It was part adoration and part vilification, and it told me I had triumphed. Full of pride and exuberance, I waited for Leo to succumb."

"Can't...Can't do it..." He sniffled. "Just can't... *Everyone* has irrational fears."

I was speechless—then I fell to the ground and shouted a menacing "Look out!"

"What! What! What is it?" Leo screeched as he dove

to the pavement to join me.

"I think I just saw Mr. Rogers."

Leo's eyeballs receded, his temples throbbed, his chin twitched, and he bit his upper lip, drawing blood. "Y-you lie," he managed to spit.

"I could be mistaken. Let's wait here and see." I smiled.

"Let's goooo!" Leo howled, pulling my arm and dragging me into the station, muttering: "It's ok, it's ok, it's ok... Some things are worse than Brooklyn...."

All the way there, despite a ten-minute delay and a thirty-five minute jarring, squealing, standing-up-because-there-were-no-seats train ride, I had a ball. I would periodically look around and stare, pretending I had spotted Mr. Rogers, and Leo would snap his head, follow my gaze, and turn green. It was amusing. But all good things must come to an end and we finally arrived at Coney. We descended and made our way to the address, which turned out to be The Church of the Living Gospel. A cadaverous giant in a green polyester leisure suit greeted us at the front door and beckoned:

"C'mon in, c'mon in. This is the place. Everyone's welcome. Gonna be some fun tonight... Yum yum."

I looked at Leo and Leo looked at me and together we grinned at each other as we entered the church through the prayer room. It was like a homecoming. Everything inside was night dark. The only light was on the dais. All I could tell as I looked around was that we were the only ones there under sixty. We took two seats in the rear and waited, and while waiting I remember how proud I felt to be an American. Where else but America could men like Pat Robertson and Jerry Fallwell, men who in another time and place would have been peasants or rum runners or Bureau of Indian Affairs land agents, where else could such men be religious leaders? And where else but the land of the home and the free and the bravado, the nation that brought us the Bill of Rights, which made legal the Old Knick, the personals in the *Swinger's Directory*, and *Bound and Gagged*, where else could The Church of the Living Gospel receive freedom of religion prerogatives and an I.R.S. tax deduction for throwing a fuckerwear bash? What a country! That's what I was thinking when the minister stepped out of his closet. He brushed back his slicked-down hair with his bejeweled hands, snapped his suspenders, and stepped onto a stool so he could be seen.

"Welcome, welcome," he intoned, "to God's little quarter acre in Brooklyn." He laughed at his own little joke, turned on a tape recorder,which miraculously managed to continue to play Bolero, and commenced with the business of the night.

"We are gathered here tonight to celebrate the spirit of the flesh—and to raise a little money for our church. Other faiths, as you know, use Bingo for this purpose, but we at The Church of the Living Gospel are opposed to this. Gambling, as the scriptures tell us, is a sin. Begetting, however, is the way of Our Lord. That is why we are gathered here tonight—to offer whatever assistance and aids modern technology can provide and to encourage you to add to the flock..." He then paused and reached under the dais. "...So what am I bid for this dildo!"

"Two dollars," Leo stood up and screeched.

"Leo," I said, yanking him back to his seat, "we have thirty-five dollars max. That's it. Let's make sure we get what we want. Agreed?"

Leo stood back up and shouted, "Two-fifty."

"Once, twice, sold to the man in the Hefty bag cape and crown."

Next came the edible undies. "Eat 'em up," laughed the minister as he held them in the air with one hand and snapped his suspenders with the other. "Sugar is good for the soul." We bought six of those, in six different, unnatural flavors. We also bought one more dildo that was shaped like Karen Silkwood and guaranteed to glow in the dark, a battery-powered vibrator that the C.I.A. had supplied to Madame Nhu, a set of brass ben wah balls—for Jean, we both agreed—and a pair of matching black leather jock straps, each with a red heart sewn on the front. Beneath the hearts, in small cursive letters, it read: "I've got this heart on for you." The only item we disagreed on was Lady MaDonna, the plastic inflatable woman. Leo wanted it and I didn't. "No way," I said. "We've already spent thirty-eight dollars. That's it. Besides, we can make our own at home with a mannequin." Reluctantly, Leo agreed.

"Hokay," announced the minister, "that about does it for tonight. Good luck and Godspeed." Then he snapped his suspenders, leaped over the dais, landed on someone in the third row, and hollered a thundering: "Orgy!" Somehow, then, inscrutably, the only light that was on turned off and Bolero became louder and louder. Immediately, Leo and I joined hands and scooped up whomever we could net and steered them into a corner sacristy. What proceeded next was a *menage a cinq*. At least I think it was *a cinq*. It may have been *a six* or *a sept*. Who could tell? What I could tell, though, was that one woman had one breast, another had no hair, and a third had hardly any teeth—unless, of course, that was Leo.

"You know," I said, as we stood on the platform waiting for the train to Manhattan, "having sex with someone is a good way to meet them."

Leo then said one of the most intelligent things I ever heard him say. It was wisdom. Gospel. More true than the Shroud of Turin. "You bet your life," he said, "but that's not the best part. The best part is the moment right after orgasm is the perfect time for truth and betrayal. You just have to know how to use it."

>>>

I wanted that night to be a breakthrough, but in no time at all Leo slipped back to his televisionary ways. He sat hunched in front of the RCA all the time now, toking, gumming his Cheetos, and rolling Jean's ben wah balls around in his palm, *a la* Queeg. Occasionally, he got confused and popped a ball into his mouth instead of a Cheeto and bit it. That's what I was waiting for as I sat with him one evening reading about the collapse of the Kansas City Hyatt's skywalk and the death of 113 people. Leo was watching a show about hunger in the sub-Sahara. "One hundred and fifty million people are going to die there," the announcer said, "during the next twelve months." I looked up as a Lean Cuisine commercial appeared and smiled when I saw the peacock. At least, I thought, Leo's taste in programming had improved as he watched only NBC now, the channel with the consistently lowest Nielson ratings and the greatest amount of violence and mayhem per second.

I was about to congratulate him on his choice of channels when his EPA hazardous-waste slicker fell off his shoulders. I gaped. He was wearing nothing now but his leather jock strap and his crown. It was more abhorrent than even I could bear. I was about to tell him so when there, on the RCA, in red, white, and blue letters, I read:

In Memorium
John Fitzgerald Kennedy, 1917-1963
on the eighteenth anniversary of his death

I shut my eyes. I was stunned. Nothing else could have shown me how much I had given up. Once, in the long ago and faraway nearby—even though I was only five years old when he got hit—that date was a date of significance, like Christmas and Easter and Halloween. On that day my orphanage would stop and remember, and we'd discuss our hearts and our souls and what we would do for our country. And every year I swore to god and Benjamin Jeffries that when I grew up, I'd make life a little bit better for someone. It sounds funny now, but it's true.... I opened my eyes—the words were still on the screen—and I shut them again to forget. Only what I wanted to forget wasn't forgettable. Time, I guess, wounds all heals.... I saw Jack Kennedy slump forward, causing the pale pink of Jackie's dress to blush, and his brains spread out on the streets of Dealey Plaza, left there for the street cleaners, tourists, and historians to pick over. I opened my eyes. At a loss of $125,000 a second, NBC kept the memorial silently on the air. I watched it and mused: who but Leo could have guessed that November 22, 1963, would not be the end of something big, but the beginning of something bigger; not a Great Society, but a Grated Society, one that would be ground from an infinity of grassy knolls and generations of textbook depository buildings? Truly, he was a prophet, a Futurist, clearly a man out of time.

"All right, already...." He was throwing Cheetos into the air and catching a few. Then he spit out a burnt one and asked, "Which one was he anyhow? The one in the kitchen or the one who drove off the bridge?"

I could hardly believe it—even from him. "Leo, you fool, he was neither. He was John Fitzgerald Kennedy, the first Catholic ever to be president of this country."

"Oh, yeah, I remember... What was the name of the guy who killed him?"

"Lee Harvey Oswald?"

"Yeah, him... And the guy who killed him?"

"Jack Ruby."

"Yeah, yeah, and the Kennedy in the kitchen?"

"Sirhan Sirhan." I was beginning to get the point. "Right," I said, "James Earl Ray killed Martin Luther King Jr. John Wilkes Booth killed Lincoln. All of them have two first names. Some of them have three. The only one who doesn't fit is the guy who killed John Lennon."

"He doesn't count," Leo bit down on a ben wah ball and howled. "He was nuts."

For the next several hours I was really impressed. Leo's stupid theory actually seemed to make sense. But later that night in bed, I had a revelation: it was I, not Leo, who knew the facts. In fact, I realized, it was always me and not Leo who knew the facts, and I understood something else as well: Leo's theories were based on literature, *The Daily News*, and instinct, not an empirical data base—and his knowledge of history was as vacuous as his knowledge of economics. That bothered me, because without knowledge of history, I knew Leo would be locked into forever repeating the past. So far it had worked for him because the past was as pernicious as the present—but that was nothing I was willing to bank on. And then, right before I fell asleep, it hit me. I was stunned as I lay in bed, my eyes open, staring at nothing, and repeating: "Leo Solomon is a name with two first names... Leo Solomon is a name with two first names...."

>>>

"There's nothing to do. Let's go to SoHo."

"Nah," Leo said. "I'm doing Jean. You go to SoHo."

I did and was utterly amazed as I entered the Hoffman Gallery. "Wow! They're showing *this*!" I was awestruck. I couldn't believe they were showing it in public. At the Old Knick, they had to blacken out the posters. "Who's the artist?" I asked the salesman.

"Judy Chicago. " He winked.

I went over to the first painting and scratched and sniffed and smelled only acrylic. I walked away disappointed. Larry Flynt could do better than this. Larry Flynt *did* do better than this! I moved on to the second painting. It was more of the same. At the third, a gargantuan black security guard in a bright red mini with a magnum strapped to her thigh, waddled over to me. "And what the hell do you think you're doing?" she said.

"Looking for Elijah," I grinned. "He's in there."

She began fingering her pistol and watching me as I wandered around the gallery, peeking. Finally, I was ready to leave. After seeing what I saw, I felt an urgency for the Old Knick, where in the spirit of the holiday season they were showing *Come All Ye Faithful, Santa's Little Helpers,* and *The Resurrection of Eve.*

I left the gallery, rushed towards the subway, and ran smack into a crowd of thirty or forty people standing on the sidewalk in front of a window, ooohing and ahhhing and groaning. I pushed my way through to peep. A man was on the other side of the window wearing black lace panties and a lady's blonde wig. He was lying on a bed and getting it on with fifty pounds of raw meat and ground hamburger. His dick was painted red and a hot dog was shoved up his ass. Someone handed me a flyer. This was Paul McCarthy's *In Sailor's Meat,* it read, sponsored by the Museum of Modern Art: MOMA, where the Samoan security guard religiously barred Leo's entry; MOMA, home of

117

Monet, Van Gogh, Cezanne, and Picasso; MOMA, the last place in the City with standards. MOMA, MOMA Mia. I turned the flyer over. Next month, it said, come watch Chris Burden get shot. I was so pleased I sat through two showings at the Old Knick and hardly remembered a thing.

Then I went home to tell Leo. He, of course, was watching TV. Somehow he had managed to change the channel. I knew that because as I walked in the announcer said it was ABC.

"What's on?" I asked.

"Nuttin."

I figured that was probably correct. I started to go to my room when the announcer said, "Stay tuned for *Love Boat.*"

"*Love* Boat!" I screeched. "*Love* Boat!" I turned around. "You're watching *Love Boat!*"

Leo shrugged.

I nodded and smiled—and kicked my foot right through the tube.

"Ha," Leo said, "now I don't have to worry about Mr. Rogers."

"That's right, and you can't watch Geraldo or Saturday morning cartoons either. Ha! Ha!" And with that, I marched out the door and headed west to watch the sun die in New Jersey.

Hours later I returned, feeling much better. What the hell, I figured, live and let die. It was X-Mas season after all, and I had nowhere else to go. Half way down the stairs, I heard Leo. His bed was squeaking and he was panting, "Do it, do it, please, again, I need it." He was in his bedroom with Jean. I quietly unlocked all of the locks, and to show him that I was no longer angry—as in let be bygones be bygones and Auld Enzymes—I stripped off my clothes, took a deep breath, and threw open his door....

"Leo," I shrieked, "I'm here!"

He jumped up, rolled over, and squirted himself in the face.

"Oh, no...." Facing me, mouth agape, her tiny tuft of hair wilting, was Lady MaDonna, the plastic inflatable woman. I was shocked. I couldn't believe Leo spent the money—and then refused to share. I stood there, stark naked, hands on hips, dong outstretched, and demanded, "What the hell are you doing?"

Leo sighed, picked up Lady MaDonna and held her. He hugged her and began to wail.

>>>

The rest of the week Leo and I prudently stayed out of each other's way. He remained in the apartment, wearing his crown and jock strap, reading *The Daily News*, wistfully gazing at the hole in the RCA. And I moped about, too, no longer my cheery self. I even went back to find Irene. But time also wounds old heels. As soon as he saw me, Pop picked up a giant rotten white fish and charged me, and Mom threw loaves of moldy bread. It was then that I made my New Year's resolution: No more fighting with Leo. I returned to the apartment as it started to rain and found him on the floor counting pennies.

"What are you doing?" I asked.

"Counting pennies."

"I can see that, Leo, but why?"

"How much money do you have?"

I looked in my pocket. "Twenty-six cents."

"Not enough."

Don't scream, I told myself, don't scream. "What for?" I casually asked.

"Betty Bimbo, you moron. It's New Year's Eve and I want to get laid."

I could certainly understand that, but between us we didn't have the $3.50. Besides, I didn't want to tell him, because it would only upset him—he owed her money from the last time, and if he didn't pay her soon, she and her mother would come up here and cut him. "What about Jean?"

"Nah. We had a fight. She got jealous of Lady MaDonna."

That I could understand, too. Not knowing what else to say, and having nothing worse to do, I went to my orange crate and sat down. In a minute, Leo did the same. Together, for about an hour, we sat there, listening to the rain, staring at the spider webs, the garbage, piles of old calendars, and the hole in the RCA. At last, I heard the sound of noisemakers. I looked up, saw Leo looking at me, was about to say nothing about something, when Leo winked at me and said, "Let's ball."

Frankly, I thought Ford had a better idea with the Edsel. This was not, I was certain, an idea whose time had come. Then again, I didn't have any reasons not to, except perhaps not wanting to mix business with pleasure, which I was sure Leo would never comprehend. Besides, I wasn't really doing anything but sitting on my orange crate, and I did, after all, make that resolution, which I knew I would have to break if I disagreed. Still, I wasn't too keen to do it, so I said as noncommittally as I could: "I don't know, Leo."

"C'mon. What do you have to lose?"

That was true, but not convincing. "What about Jean?"

"Jean who?"

What else could I say? Hand in hand, we went off to Leo's room. Suffice it to say, it was every bit the pain in the ass that it's cracked up to be and not at all half bad. Afterwards, I struggled to get up and make my way back to my bed, but I couldn't get out from under Leo. A few minutes later I fell asleep.

"Luth," Leo groaned in my ear.

"Huh? What?" I pushed myself away from him again.

His head fell off my shoulder and landed facing mine. He looked awful. He exhaled. He smelled worse. I held my breath and turned away, but even breathing through my mouth I couldn't sleep. I recounted the news of the year: 1 pope shot, 4 nuns, 1 Egyptian prime minister, and 1 president; 24 kids strangled in Atlanta, 84 gamblers burned in Vegas, and 113 tea dancers crushed in Kansas City; 10,000 more species expired, 150,000,000 Africans starved, 800,000,000 refugees, and a zillion professional ear slicings, finger removals, knee cappings, genital probes, rapes, beatings, executions and disappearances, not to mention the first baseball strike in history. My eyes were getting drowsy. I began to count countries currently at war—Afghanistan, the Soviet Union, Iran, Iraq, Israel, Nicaragua, Angola, El Salvador, South Africa, Lebanon, Syria, Cambodia, Viet Nam, China, Cuba, Ireland, England, Argentina, Botswana, Rhodesia, Chad, Zambia, Tanzania, Zaire, Mozambique, Mauritania, Laos, Equador, Uruguay, Uganda, Pakistan, Thailand, India, Saudi Arabia, Turkey—and was proud to note that in almost every case both sides were receiving U.S. aid, advice, and dollars.

"Luth!" Leo kicked and screamed, threw his arm over me, hugged me, and humped.

My heart shrank. My testicles shriveled. I oozed out from under him and stared, mortified, as he sucked on his yellowed sheet. I couldn't believe it. Never in my life did I expect it. Anything else I could have put up with: his not sharing Lady MaDonna; his lack of knowledge about history and economics; his watching TV—even *Love Boat*, especially now that the set was smashed; his fear of Mr. Rogers; his provincialism; the maybe not-so-stupid theory about two first names; *The Daily News*; anything, anything, but this.... The *L word*.... *That* affirmation! I felt trifled with. I picked up the hard-bound collected works of Freud, clobbered

123

him and left.

Outside, it was still raining—only harder now and colder. I scurried to the neighborhood Chock Full O' Nuts, threw open the door, and instantly understood how it got its name. Each and every stooped-shouldered-stool-slumping denizen of the night looked as if he and/or she had been hit by all of the ten plagues at once. It was awesome. Talk about your counter culture! Even more awesome was the transvestite with a mustache from the Y who remembered me. He winked. I waved and ordered my coffee to go.

As I headed weat towards New Jersey, I knew what had to be done. I just had to muster the courage to leave. I sloshed on, head down, sipping coffee, getting soaked by those proverbial buckets of water when I heard something crash and shatter. I looked up. A block away, one by one, just like the Rockettes, the windows popped out of Leo's building: they just waited their turn and went boom. Was it an omen? Did it mean anything? Could Leo be right about other things? I sat in a puddle and thought. Across the street, the transvestite leaned against a window and waited.

In no time at all, I had an "Aha." Leo was warning me—about windows, buildings, himself. That was why he said it was everybody and everything that was doing itself and the rest of us in: the art world, the religious world, musicians, parents, teachers, doctors, athletes, scientists, all political parties and persuasions, businessmen, television, newspapers, movies, lovers, lawyers, and every level of government from the rural town planning board to multinational states. And yes, even Leo, which was why he said don't trust anyone with two first names even as he knew he had two. And why he said *everyone* caused it to be this way, because it included him. And why he said the time after orgasm was perfect for betrayal and truth. Wow! Things suddenly all made sense, everything from mea culpa, mea culpa, mea maxima culpa to *In Sailor's Meat* being sponsored by MOMA.

Still, I wasn't too sure. Leo or Newark, that was the choice. Across the street, the transvestite waved. I waved back. He jumped, and I leaped. Behind him was a poster of Hunter Thompson, Dr. Gonzo himself. I epiphanied right in my pants. "Luth," I whispered, trying it out. "Luth," I said louder to hear it. "Luth! Luth! Luth!" I screamed! That was it! Leo never said the four-letter L word. He said *loathe*. Or *loath*. Or both. The sumofabitch was a genius.

On my way home I looked for a clock, but the storm had knocked them all out. Real clocks with arms that moved in circles no longer seemed to exist. Everything now was digital—and blank. There was no way to know if it was early or late, pre-or postdiluvial. I turned the final corner onto our block and was greeted by a postmodern ecumenical site: all of the trees were down, every car window had been smashed, glass was all over the concrete; police cars sirened and flashed; wires sparkled and fizzed; and graffiti was on everything in at least thirteen different languages and all of the primary colors. There was no doubt about it: the writing was on the wall. Every parking meter had its neck broken and proclaimed itself Expired. Leo was oblivious to it all. He was sitting on his bed wrapped in Lady MaDonna's arms wearing his crown, holding his head, looking bruised, gaunt, and frog-eyed, staring at the collected works of Freud.

"Where were you?" he asked.

"Killing time," I said.

"Good," he responded. "Get some for me."

I smiled and took my clothes off. Leo watched me and raised the blanket. I slid into bed and pushed against him.

"Yow!" Leo howled, "You're cold!" I laughed and nuzzled in closer. Leo pulled the blanket higher and over our heads. It was perfect. To survive, we would become invisible. The Enlightenment was over and out.

>>>

This is our arrangement. We have been living it now for years: I read about the past (as backwards is now longer than forwards); Leo reads about the present (He thinks history is rust); Lady MaDonna sits on her crate, mouth open, in a state of perpetual awe. None of us has a future. That is what keeps us together. Like this evening when Leo looked up from his reading of the latest atrocity and grinned, and I grinned too, and Lady MaDonna nodded because this is the way the world ends, this is the way the world ends, this is the way the world ends, not with a whimper but a band.... And the band plays on, though the party is over and the jig is up.

What we have is each other together alone.

About the Author

First born Jewish son after the Holocaust, that story.

First generation American, that story too.

From city to suburbs, Brooklyn to Long Island, near poor to near rich, then rocketing downward mobility. From organized labor (sewing trades on mother's side, restaurant trade on father's), to teacher (mom) and lawyer (dad), to marginalized labor again: part-time teacher until age 40 (no benefits, no retirement, no money), then full-time, tenured teacher, and marginalized writer of fiction and memoir.

Union leader: officer, worker, activist in American Federation of Teachers.

Civil Rights: marched, picketed, arrested, spoke-out; present at the "I Have a Dream" speech and the Apollo Theater.

Anti-Vietnam War: marched, picketed, arrested, resisted, screamed-out; present at numerous marches on Washington; threw garbage can through a window at the State Department, proving that even then I understood and appreciated the power of metaphor.

Anti draft and anti draft counseling.

Vista Volunteer in Washington, D.C., where I was paid by the Office of Economic Opportunity to organize tenants against the Federal Housing Authority, who threatened to beat me up.

Vista Volunteer in Greensboro, North Carolina, where I was paid to teach poor people how to save and spend their money. Organized them instead in an interracial tenants union so they could save more money, which they then used to buy guns to protect themselves from each other.

Freedom of Information Act, 25 page FBI file. Agents spent most of their time trying to figure out if I was really married. I was, but they could never seem to verify it. My wife, however, had no trouble either verifying it or dissolving it, as she was always better and smarter and more vigilant than they.

Left New York in 1962 to go to school in Madison, Wisconsin. Left Madison in 1968 with two degrees, a teaching credential, a wife, and an unplanned honeymoon detention in Chicago jail during the Democratic National Convention. Spent first night at Lincoln Park with Rubin, Hoffman, piglet, and Yippies. Spent the second night in jail. The third night I was in George McGovern's suite in the Sheraton Blackstone, watching it on TV, all of which helped to contribute to a profound sense and appreciation of the absurd.

Went to Greensboro, North Carolina, and taught

history and political science at a black university from 1968-70. I was visited by the FBI. The school was visited by the KKK and the National Guard. One student killed.

Came to Berkeley, California, in 1970, right after People's Park and Kent State. Still married, unemployed, living on welfare, and food stamps. Accepted at law school, decided not to go, and began working on a reader of Social Conflict Theory as well as a political science teacher's manual and two political science textbooks. Came face to face with feminism and lost. Happy I can still walk and have kids.

Started teaching history and political science at Merritt College in Oakland, birthplace of the Black Panther Party and Huey Newton and Bobby Seale. Did that until 1977-8 when I got a National Endowment for the Humanities grant to start an oral history project, a la Studs Terkel, which got me involved in working with older people, which led to my next job and an interest in stories and storytelling.

Went to Vista College in Berkeley and set up one of the largest and most comprehensive older adult education programs in the nation. Had over 150 classes in five towns, over 100 teachers, a budget of half million dollars, and over 5,000 students in 1982. Taught well elderly, frail elderly, people who were working with elderly and people who wanted to work with elderly. Program was dismantled thanks to our Republican friends in Sacramento, who later went to Washington and did to the country what they'd already done to the State.

I moved on to other things: labor union work for teachers (my day job) and graduate school in English and creative writing (at night). What I had finally learned was the line between truth and fiction is porous. I realized that fact and data mean nothing until they are interpreted and once they are interpreted they are no longer fact and data, but fiction. So I asked myself, why write lies that are pretending to be truths when I can discover truths by making up lies? The answer led me to fiction. That and working with old folks, hearing their stories and learning that all stories are unique and the same. Very humiliating and freeing to realize everything has already happened to someone somewhere and everything for each of us is also brand new.

About stories: once when I was very young my grandfather gave me a dollar and told me to go to the store and buy him a packet of cigarettes. I bought a dollar's worth of candy instead and came back and told him. He spanked me and sent me to my room. Clearly, it would have gone better had I a story to tell.

Years later when I got expelled from high school when a teacher caught me doing something I shouldn't have been doing and heard me say, "You fuck," I knew I'd better come up with a tale. So I told my mother I said, "What luck." She, mother of first-born Jewish son after the holocaust, believed me, defended me, was shocked when I finally confessed. So I learned another lesson, a lesson repeated again and again after the U-2, Vietnam, Watergate, the Contras, Irangate, Monica Lewinsky, and WMD: a story that's true is better than one that is false.

So I began writing fictions and creating lies to discover my truths. Hence, a collection of stories, *I Saw a Man Hit His Wife*.

And then I went to France, the old world, where everything is new to me, including me. I got married again and wrote, *I'll Never Be French(no matter what I do)* and *(Not Quite) Mastering the Art of French living*. Then I wrote this.

And here I am.

www.markgreenside.com

www.ingramcontent.com/pod-product-compliance
Lightning Source LLC
LaVergne TN
LVHW021351080426
835508LV00020B/2231